33 Years on the Street

Living With and Through

Physical Abuse &

Ineffective Psychiatry

by
Marshall Friedell

Table of Contents

1.

Parents

After I received a medical misdiagnosis in 1958, my life was spent watching traffic, living a life of hopelessness. It all began with the abuse I suffered at the hands of my parents.

I was born on April 16, 1936, the son of Harry and Florence Friedell. My parents were immigrants who both came from Russia in 1921 and settled in Minneapolis near the north side. I have a younger sister, Roselyn, who was born on May 4, 1941.

My parents' lives were shattered by the pogroms, the Russian Revolution, and the First World War. I once asked Mom what the pogroms were all about. She told me the Cossacks were running up and down the street shouting, "Kill the Jews."

"What did you do then?" I asked.

"We ran down the stairs to the basement to hide until they passed."

My maternal grandfather was a meat cutter and had his own butcher shop with my grandmother occasionally helping out. I once asked my sister if Mom's life in Russia had anything to do with the way Mom treated me. In Roselyn's opinion, it was yes. Mom always told me that much of her life in Russia was portrayed in *Dr. Zhivago*.

I told my sister of some people I know who survived

the holocaust. They raised a beautiful family that included three sons, all medical doctors. One does general surgery, another is an ear, nose, and throat specialist, and the third is a cardiologist. To these two Holocaust survivors, their children were of primary importance to them, unlike my parents.

The Russian people are very musically minded and my grandparents were no different. Mom's forte was the piano. I remember Mom telling me that when she was scheduled for a lesson, grandfather took out his last dollar bill to pay for that lesson. Mom also loved dogs. As a young child, she had a dog named Marsik who was very loyal to her. After grandfather's service in the Russian Army during the First World War, both grandparents concluded that times would never get better. History was to prove them right. It was time to leave.

By this time one of Mom's aunts had married and settled down in Minneapolis. Upon hearing of the family's desire to emigrate, she sent money to enable the family to leave. But in 1920, Russia sealed off her borders and no one was allowed to leave. Still, my grandparents were determined to do so. They enlisted the help of farmers in the countryside, who were grandfather's customers, to hide the family during the day to enable them to cross rivers and streams during the night. They did so under a hail of bullets. Their lives were in danger.

They traveled on to Warsaw, Poland, which, in later years, Mom called the most beautiful city she had ever seen. While in Warsaw, Mom learned to speak Polish. It intrigued me very much that a young 16-year-old could pick up a foreign language so fast without being schooled in it.

They lived in Warsaw for about a year, then traveled

to Liverpool, England and then went through Canada to come to America to settle in Minneapolis.

Because America did not let married couples in, Aunt Clara and Uncle Max stayed in Winnipeg. They had three children, Rose, Daniel, and Jack. I believe Jack still lives there.

While coming to America, the Bubonic Plague broke out and passengers were quarantined for two weeks. Upon coming to Minnesota, Mom went to stay with Aunt Sadie and her second husband, Sam, in South St. Paul. While there, she went to work at both the Swift and Armour Packing houses. The way she told it, the work she did was piecework and she always prided herself on being able to outperform her brother Ben, who also worked there. Eventually, my grandfather taught Uncle Ben the meat-cutting trade.

Since Mom was adept at piano playing and piecework, I believe that one of the failures of my grandparents was not encouraging her to pursue a career in piano, either as a teacher or player. She should have gone on to obtain a high school diploma and a college degree in that field. Instead, when she moved in with my grandparents, she went to work in a sweatshop—a laundry. In those days there was no air conditioning and Mom would tell of young girls passing out from the heat.

Mom said she always stood her ground. She was born with a good pair of hands and was never encouraged to make use of them. Shame on my grandparents. I am certain that my life would have been much better had Mom pursued a college education.

At this point I must take a moment and observe what happened to the Jewish people in the world of ours as recorded in history. In Egypt, a Pharaoh decided to drown at birth every Jewish male infant. The Romans almost succeeded. The Spanish Inquisition did not help the Jews. The Jew was the scapegoat in many countries in central Europe for many generations. The infamous Nazis tried in our generation, and almost succeeded, to wipe out the Jews. The Russian Tsar Nicholas I tried a new way of genocide; he ordered all Jewish boys at age 12 to be inducted into the Army for 25 years. Many of the boys died, some were converted to Christianity, others came home suffering various forms of disability.

Dad was born in St. Petersburg, Russia, the third oldest child, on July 5, 1905. He had one brother Nathan, and two sisters, Clara and Tobey. His father, Morris Friedell, passed away, apparently of a heart attack, when Dad was only three. The story goes that Dad woke up one morning and started crying and when grandfather went to attend to Dad's needs, grandfather dropped dead. I believe my grandmother physically abused my father throughout their stay in Russia because she blamed him for that tragedy. Dad was only 5'2", which tells me that she deprived him of some food. What physical means grandmother used I will never know.

I am certain that had Dad never been abused, he wouldn't have abused me. Studies have shown that abuse runs in families and it was my misfortune to have a father like him.

After grandfather's death, Dad's older brother Nathan went to live with their grandparents. Their grandmother wanted him with them for two reasons. One was to make it easier for their widowed mother, and the other was to watch over Nathan so that he observed the Prayer of Kaddish for his father. This is a Jewish custom; the male children say Kaddish for their parents who died. They say it twice a day for one year and also on the anniversary of the day of death. Grandmother also wanted Uncle Nate to attend religious school to learn much of the Jewish religion.

Shortly after arriving in Minneapolis, Dad attended night school, not only to learn the English language, but to study American history. After completing his studies at night school, he enrolled at Dunwoody Industrial Institute to pursue a career as an electrician. After a time at Dunwoody he dropped out.

I thought it was a result of a language barrier, but my sister Roselyn said that Dad had to support my grandmother. Here you have a case similar to my mother's situation. Here is a son who wants to better himself, but his mother stands in his way. I can't help but think how much better my sister and I would have been had both my parents pursued careers in piano and electricity. Would they have physically abused us?

By this time Uncle Nathan—who was taught the produce business by his Uncle Harry, whom he lived with—opened up his own produce business, which consisted of eggs and chickens. His uncle filed bankruptcy and, as a result, a family feud ensued, which has never ended.

Uncle Nathan called his business Nathan's Produce. After several business failures, Dad went to work for his brother as an egg candler. Egg candling is done by taking an individual egg and putting it up to the light in a lantern. This is to see if there are any spots like blood in the egg. The business was unionized, which would work in Dad's favor as the years passed by.

Dad was in the 1934 Truck Driver strike that resulted in four deaths with the Minnesota National Guard being called out to quell the disturbances.

* * * * * *

After their marriage, Mom and Dad moved in with my maternal grandparents in North Minneapolis. My parents made two huge mistakes in their lifetime together. One was going to work for a relative and the other was moving in with my grandparents. They lived in filthy surroundings with my grandfather spitting on the floor constantly. Dad complained to Mom to no avail. My grandparents brought filthy conditions to America. They knew very little about sanitation. None of them mastered the English language; they spoke only Yiddish and, in later years, spoke Russian when they didn't want me to know what they were discussing. I believe this was a mistake as it made me erode the confidence I had in them.

We lived with my grandparents for five years when Dad, at Uncle Dave's urging, bought a house at 1335 Vincent Avenue N in Minneapolis. After we moved into our own house, I started at Willard Elementary School in September 1941. I couldn't speak a word of English. This, I firmly believe, caused me to stutter. I was sent to a speech therapist who told me to speak slowly. It helped. This should have sent a signal to my parents of what the future could hold for me, but they ignored it.

The home my parents bought was ill-suited to our needs. It had no garage and an unfinished attic. The mortgage was held by my Uncle Nathan at 2%. Right after we moved in, the city made us put in a new sidewalk. My parents should have noticed the condition of the sidewalk and deducted the cost of fixing it from the asking price of $4,600.

One snowy winter day, part of the roof caved in right above the bedroom. Luckily it did not go through the ceiling. It seems that a plate was not put down to hold a rafter, causing it to crash under the weight of the snow. The house was built in 1925 and the question I have is, where was the building inspector?

I believe that Dad suffered from manic-depression disorder in which he had mood swings. Mom called them "spells." I can't remember when the physical abuse started, but when he came home and Mom told him that I misbehaved, he would take off his belt and start swinging at me, backing me into a corner where I could not escape. Mostly I was hit with the leather part, but sometimes I was hit with the metal buckle. I can't remember the physical pain associated with those beatings, but I will never forget the look on Dad's face. He was a man with a purpose—his eyes were closed, his lips were tightly sealed—he was going to get many swings, come what may.

During these attacks, Mom would yell "he has it coming," taking years off my life. After several swings at me, Mom would change her tone and scream "enough, enough." My sister got it several times, too, but I got it mostly. A few weeks before Mom passed, I talked to her about the abuse; she told me I had it coming because I irritated Dad. Then she yelled out, "So what do you want me to do?"

These attacks played a large part in my declining mental health, which resulted in my spending 33 years on the street watching traffic, living a life of hopelessness.

I don't know what joy it brings to parents to involve their children in that type of abuse.

The only time I ever got close to Dad was during the High Holiday of Rosh Hashanah and Yom Kippur. We sat together during those services. When we lived with my grandparents and Uncle Ben, I remember how Uncle Ben constantly kissed me. I remember how his beard pushed against my cheek. I never got that sign of love from Dad.

In my opinion, he didn't know how to be a father since he lost his own father when he was only three years old. I was always ashamed of being with Dad because of his height, 5'2", and the type of work he did, which was egg candling.

Another signal of my emotional state occurred when I was bar mitzvahed. I broke out in a rash. Both my parents ignored it as a passing phenomenon. It didn't mean a thing to them. Not even a warning sign that I needed extra help in growing up.

We did not have a family car. I begged my parents to buy a car, but they flatly refused. Whenever they needed transportation of any kind, Uncle Nathan would let Dad have the pickup truck on the condition that he would go to the shop and feed the chickens on Sunday mornings. A couple of times when Dad had the truck, he tried to teach me how to drive. We'd go to the farmers market at Glenwood and Lyndale, not far from where he worked. What an experience. I had trouble with the clutch and he would yell and scream at me. Imagine how I felt. I should have gotten out and walked home. You don't learn under those circumstances.

I will always feel I could have had an easier time growing up had we had a family car. It would have helped me to come out of my "shell" to be able to date and to be one of the boys.

In 1947, Minneapolis had a city-wide X-ray program where people could go to get free chest X-rays. They had mobile X-ray units strategically located throughout the city. For a while before that, Mom noticed that Dad's health was declining, so she urged him to get an X-ray, which they both did. The unit was located at 17th and Vincent just four blocks from where we lived. Mom's X-ray turned out okay, but no so for Dad. He was referred for a follow-up and after various procedures, including a biopsy, he was diagnosed with Hodgkin's disease, a treatable, but incurable cancer.

When Uncle Nathan found out that it was a fatal disease, he wanted to fire Dad, but Dad went to the Union and the Union told Uncle Nathan that they would close him down if he followed through with his threat. What a way to treat an employee, let alone your brother.

At that time, my paternal grandmother was living in a nursing home in St. Paul. Two weeks before Dad died, Uncle Nathan forced him to go to apply for medical assistance for her. Based on Uncle Nathan's wealth, he knew he could not get it, so he forced my dad to apply under the threat of making Dad help out paying her way. She lived in St. Paul, Ramsey County, and Dad mistakenly went to Minneapolis, Hennepin County, to apply. Dad had just undergone radiation for Hodgkin's. I remember skin peeling off his neck as a result. When I got home, he opened the door to let me in and I thought I was going to drop dead. Whenever he took sick, he would leave work and come home. This occurred around six months after he completed radiation. I have often asked myself how Uncle Nathan could force a brother who is dying to apply for welfare. Especially when Uncle Nathan had the financial means to pay for grandmother's stay in a long-term facility.

Two weeks later, on February 3, 1955, Dad died at age 49. What a blow! Mom got a call around 1:00 p.m. saying that Dad had a heart attack and was being transported to General Hospital. When they got to the hospital, Uncle Nathan's son Stuart was in the hallway and told Mom to sit down and he gave her the news that Dad had passed.

When she got home she told me "you don't have a dad anymore."

I remember when I was saying Kaddish, Uncle Nathan, who was a member of a different congregation, came to services at my synagogue and sat next to me. After the services were over, I broke down and cried my heart out. As I was to learn later on, Uncle Nathan had a terrible dream that night about how shabbily he had treated Dad.

In the summer of 1958, three years after Dad's passing, I came home at 9:00 p.m. I wanted to turn on the television to watch the 10:00 p.m. news. Mom kept telling me not to watch the news. But I did turn on the t.v. and I found out why she discouraged me from watching. The news anchor reported that a Nathan Friedell went swimming in Cedar Lake and drowned. For many years I thought that Uncle Nathan did a foolish thing by going swimming before the lifeguards came on duty and not using the buddy system since he had suffered several heart attacks. He always did foolish things and I thought this was one of them.

But I recently heard from my cousin Blanche of what really happened that day. Uncle Nathan sensed a heart attack coming on so he drove his car into the lake, which was only a half a block from his home, and committed suicide.

My cousin Stuart took over the business and it became known as Crystal Farm Foods. Over several years, Mom would plead with Dad to go into the produce business, but he refused to do that. He knew enough of the business to be an outstanding competitor.

Mom was a very difficult person to communicate with. There was very little overlap in our conversations. Many times when I felt I needed help with some matter, she would tell me outright, "Don't come to me, you have got a sick father; the way you make your bed that's the way you will sleep in it." I was left to grow up on my own. I tried, but I failed. It didn't get much better with Dad either.

Then there was the physical abuse. Mom was instrumental in starting the abuse when she told Dad that I had misbehaved. What hurts me the most is how accommodating my parents, especially Mom, were to my aunts and uncles.

Mom sent money to Uncle Max and Aunt Clara because they did not want to work and when I asked her why she did it, she said, "They were starving." I said, let them go to work. She kept silent. She could not give me credit to say I was right. She never understood the meaning of LOVE. It just meant food to her. I, too, was starving for love, affection, a pat on the back, and constructive criticism to become a contributing member of society. For most parents, this is asking very little, but for my parents, it was asking too much.

Mom's philosophy of life was "you have to do it yourself." What she didn't understand was that no man is an island unto himself. I suffered from that philosophy, resulting in spending 33 years on the street believing I was schizophrenic.

Before Mom passed, she wanted to marry me off so I would not be alone. I go back to when I turned 16 and begged and pleaded with both parents to get a family car. They refused. I really do believe that, with a car, I could have come out of my shell, dated, and had close friends. Both parents never thought of what the future held for me. They couldn't have cared less. I remember when I asked Mom to call a neighbor, Mrs. Weinberg, who had just returned from the hospital diagnosed with diabetes to ask how she was getting along. Mom started jumping up and down, tearing at her hair, turning red in the face and screaming that I didn't care for her. It terrified me.

Years ago, I got a part-time temporary job as a recruiter for a blood pressure study, which was collaboration between the old Mount Sinai Hospital and the University of Minnesota School of Public Health's Epidemiology Department. At the beginning of the study, I was getting paid, but because I was on disability, I later requested to become a volunteer, which was granted. At the end of the study, unbeknownst to me, they surprised me by throwing a party for me. I was elated that somebody like me would be the beneficiary of such an honor. When I came home, I told Mom about the surprise. She sat back in the chair and yelled out to me, "You?!" She couldn't bring herself to say, "I am happy for you" or "they see the same good attributes that I see in you."

Then there was the time one winter when a heavy snowstorm hit Minneapolis. I went out to help my neighbors push their cars out of the snow bank. When I came in, she started yelling at me for helping them out, to the point of not giving me supper. She was seething with anger. Why? She couldn't praise me for my helping attitude. She didn't have it in her.

Another time occurred when Mom broke her hip and required surgery. This occurred on a Saturday afternoon. After she was admitted, the surgeon came in her room and introduced herself. At that time I didn't know what was going on in Mom's mind. The surgery was scheduled for 9:00 a.m. the next day, a Sunday. As I wanted to see her before she went into surgery, I got there around 8:30. I was astounded when she barked out at me that she did not want that doctor to operate on her because she felt the doctor was too young. The time was 8:45 and the operating room had called that they were ready. Luckily, her internist was making rounds and he convinced her to have the surgery. The nurses thought I had put her up to it. Nothing could be further from the truth.

I remember when I bought a life insurance policy. Mom was steadfastly against it. A few months before she passed at age 100, she asked me, "Marshall, how much life insurance do I have?" She never thought about tomorrow, only about today, the here and now.

Still there were many things I have to give her credit for. Her work ethic overwhelmed me. She took on the burden of being the family's breadwinner after Dad passed, even though friends and relatives suggested she go on welfare. She took a job at the Dayton Co. in food services. Lately I was thinking that Mom should have gotten a job at Minneapolis Honeywell as an assembler because of her dexterity.

Two more examples of Mom's indifference to my dilemma occurred when I got laid off at Minnesota Care. I told her that I was thinking of giving a donation to the University of Minnesota if I could get a job there. The University pays into the same pension fund that State employees pay into. University employees enjoy the same benefits as do state employees, plus if they work at least 30 hours a week, the employees don't pay any tuition for one class, even depending on the workload and taking time off to go to that class.

At that time, I felt it was a win-win situation. The way I tried to explain it to Mom was that I would go to a fundraiser for a certain college or program and would contribute $1,000 in exchange for them writing me a letter of recommendation. The contribution would start after six months and be fully paid up at the end of twelve months. When I went to Mom to discuss the matter, she started yelling and hollering at me saying I would give money and not get the job. I never said that. I would get the job, and after six months start to make money payments to fulfill my pledge. This is another example of her negative treatment of me.

She never cared about tomorrow, only today—the here and now. Over the years, I have asked myself if both my parents had known that I would spend 33 years on the street overwhelmed with fear, would they have physically abused me? The answer is an absolute yes.

2.

Sports

For sixteen years, sports were a big factor in my life. As a shy withdrawn kid, sports kept me in touch with the outside world and out of reach of my parents' negative treatment of me. My connection to sports started in May of 1948 while I was attending Willard Elementary School in north Minneapolis. A classmate of mine, Jimmy Harrison, told me about the coach of his baseball team, Selmer Swanson. The coach didn't allow any foul language while playing or practicing ball. This, and other of his attributes, sounded great to me, so I went along with Jimmy to my first practice at North Commons Park. I didn't know anything about baseball; at that time, television was just emerging and I had never gone with my parents to watch the Minneapolis Millers—a triple-farm ball club owned by the then New York Giants.

I am left-handed and, would you believe it, not knowing better, I tried out for short stop. I had a Ball Hawk Glove, which was popular in those days; instead of having four fingers and a thumb, it had three fingers with large webbing between the thumb and the other fingers. I remember putting my mother's powder glove in my mitt to keep the sting of the ball to a minimum when it hit my glove.

Selmer coached three divisions of the Northside Athletic Club: Cubs, Midgets, and Juniors, depending on age. I soon found out, much to my disappointment, that being left-handed, I could not play any other position besides first base, pitcher, and outfielder. Furthermore, I did not have the natural ability to play the game since I couldn't hit, run, field, or throw.

Still, I loved the game and, as a team manager, I had the time of my life. There was always room for me. Among my assigned duties were keeping score, which included shouting out the batting order at the beginning of the inning, backing up the pitcher during batting practice, and making sure foul balls hit during practice were returned to the field as it helped keep the budget in a positive mode.

The coach was married and his wife's first name was Goldie. We called her a baseball widow because Selmer was so tied down with running three clubs, and having three sons: Billy, Donnie, and one name I can't recall. Billy and Donnie were both educators. Billy in the St. Paul school system, and Donnie as a principal in a Rochester, MN public school. Billy, besides playing baseball, also played hockey at North High School and the University of Minnesota. Selmer proudly served in the U.S. Navy in both World Wars and was employed by the U.S. Postal Service as a clerk. He took a lot of time off work to coach us kids. He had an amazing work ethic that related to the members of his ball clubs.

In 1949, the Northside A.C.'s, as they were called, were runners-up to the Minnesota State Championship in the junior division. In the 16 years I was associated with Park Board baseball; it was the greatest ball club I ever saw play the game. Dick Naylor was the starting pitcher and could play any position on the team, including catcher. I remember him having the bases loaded with nobody out and a 3-0 count on the hitter; getting him out followed by getting the next two hitters out enabled them to advance to the state tournament at the old Nicollet Ball Park in July of 1949, which was sponsored by the Minneapolis Aquatennial.

The rest of the starting lineup included Jack Rowles, who was a catcher and went on to become an all-state basketball player at Minneapolis DeLaSalle High School; Doug Gillen was a left-handed first basemen; Dick Dorf was at second base; Jimmy Ullom (I occasionally ran into him when I worked at a plumbing supply company; Jimmy was a plumber); Bob Zafala, the third baseman, who I believe was killed in the Korean War; Gilbert Hanson, a left-handed left fielder; Pete Badali, center fielder, who Selmer would always say liked to run; and Junior Wahl, the right fielder. The rest of the squad included Stanley Burnstein, whom we affectionately called Pee Wee, and a pitcher who I remember couldn't hit a lick even during batting practice. The rest of the club included Micky Bearman, Cliff Fraser, Delano McKay (who later came down with spinal meningitis while playing football at North), and Dick Schultz.

When North was in a city playoff game at the old Nicollet Ball Park, Pee Wee, with a bat in his hands, would pound the back of the dugout shouting out in Yiddish "give it a klop its," which meant hit the ball.

There are many stories I can tell about Selmer. I remember Selmer coaching a team and, on that particular Saturday morning, Tommy Fern (who played on one of Selmer's teams) was calling balls and strikes. Selmer's team was losing and Selmer was riding Tommy pretty hard. After the game Tommy ran as hard and as fast to his home, which was down the street from the diamond, with Selmer vigorously pursuing him down the street shouting "Tommy, Tommy," but to no avail.

I remember one year that, at an American Legion baseball game with Selmer coaching, Wally Irwin was on first base. I was sitting next to Selmer and he put on the steal sign. He would rub his right hand on my knee. The problem was that Wally did not catch the signal. Selmer kept rubbing my knee and the longer it took for Wally to catch the steal signal, the harder Selmer kept pounding my knee. I was a victim of the bench and I don't remember if Wally ever caught the signal.

Another instance occurred when Selmer, who had a 1932 two-door Chevrolet, loaded thirteen ball players into his car. There was no room for the equipment so he put the equipment on his fenders and off we went out to Longfellow Park, which was located near the Lake Street Bridge in far away south Minneapolis. I remember going out with them in the car and Selmer stopping on occasion to adjust the equipment lying on his car fender. It started out as a beautiful day, but later, it turned cloudy and started to rain and the game had to be cancelled. Selmer gave some of us money, including myself, to enable us to take the old streetcar home. We waited out the rain at what I believe was a Texaco Oil station called Glen's.

I remember when Selmer didn't have his car available and had a ball game scheduled, he took the team with the equipment on a Sunday afternoon on the old streetcars that they had running those days from North Commons to Phelps Field in south Minneapolis.

I made many friends during those 16 years in baseball, which I have relished all my life. Selmer left baseball in 1953 after winding up his stint with the Northside American Legion Post #230 baseball club. I believe he was forced out by the athletic director for reasons I will never know. After Selmer left baseball, he became director of skiing for the Minneapolis Park Board. I last saw Selmer at Al Ber-man's funeral service many years ago and rode with him in the procession to the cemetery in New Hope.

Selmer passed away in 1985 at the age of 85. I will always regret not visiting him while he was hospitalized, even though I knew about it. He deserved my visit to at least make him feel I was concerned about him. I also regret not attending his funeral when he passed away. I did, however, send the family a sympathy card. Selmer was like a father to me and I will never forget him.

Among the other friends I made was Dwayne Smith, who played center field for Selmer's "B" squad. I will never forget him coming to the park with a bat on his shoulder and his glove hanging by the strap on the bat. He often showboated his center field prowess by putting his glove behind his back while catching a fly ball hit in his direction. He was an outstanding basketball player at North and went on to play college basketball at Gustavus Adolphus College in St. Peter, MN. As I remember, he had the biggest pair of hands that I have ever seen on any person. I lost contact with him after we both graduated in 1954 from North.

Another friend I met through baseball was Bob Soltis, who went on to play football at the University of Minnesota as a halfback, and later on professionally with the old Boston Patriots. His career ended at a young age because of a kidney injury. I remember him running for a touchdown in a high school football game when one of his shoes came off and he lost his balance, losing a touchdown, and eventually North lost that game. He constantly kept telling me "Marsh, you know I'm the greatest," and I in turn said to him, "I know that Bob." He was a sincere person. As an example, he and I went up to north to watch a scrimmage. Bob was able to jump over the fence and he apologized to me for leading me to that fence even though he knew I couldn't jump over it.

Then there was Bill Patterson, whom we called Shorty because of his height—6'6". He was an outstanding high school basketball player who played center on the North team. I can't remember if he participated in track or not. He later went to Gustavus Adolphus College along with Dwayne Smith. Last I heard, Shorty was employed by the Minneapolis Park in a recreation position at North Commons Park. I remember I was polishing some basketballs in the equipment room at North when Shorty came up to me and said I will be rewarded. I'm still waiting for that reward.

The basketball coach at North High in those years was John Jacobi, who taught architectural drawing. He was my homeroom teacher. There are many stories I could write about "Jake," as we called him, during the time I spent at North. His team was playing at the old Minneapolis Auditorium. During a time-out, he substituted a reserve player. In those days players wore sweatpants over their shorts. Problem was that if the player forgot to put on his shorts, when he took off his sweatpants, he was not dressed from the waist down to his ankles. That's what happened to one of the reserve players. There were a couple of thousand people in attendance. Everyone started laughing and Jake could not figure out what was happening until fans started pointing at the player.

Jake was a nifty dresser. I had a front-row seat in homeroom, and one time he was polishing his shoes. Donnie Goldberg, who was seated in the next row and a few seats behind, called out to me to watch the shoe-shining event. Apparently Jake heard us talking and laughing and later at practice, he asked me, "What were you and Goldberg laughing about?"

When North lost a playoff game to end the season, Jake wrote on the clubroom blackboard "Let's not talk about basketball." Jake was married but had no children. He did, however, have pen pals.

I ran into Jake some time ago at the Normandy Hotel at a reunion of the Pill House with Judge Eugene Minenko as the emcee. Jake was in a nursing home in southeastern Minnesota when he came up to Minneapolis to attend the reunion. He was seated at the head table and stared at me and I stared back. We recognized each other immediately.

The baseball coach at North was Jim Treglawny, who taught history and eventually became an assistant principal at Minneapolis Central High School. I remember him kicking Don Cassidy out of class. Don was an outstanding athlete, being named most valuable football player in the Minneapolis football conference in 1952. Jim at that time was an assistant football coach under Rube Johnson. Jim knew quite a bit about football and very little about baseball. Word around school was that Rube, who knew baseball and less about football, would have had better success in handling the baseball team and Jim would have had better success in handling the football team. Sadly, this never happened.

I traveled with the athletic team I was privileged to be associated with. My first journey with the team was in 1951 when we went to the Minnesota State Prison in Stillwater, a maximum security facility housing between 900-1,000 inmates, to play their team, The Sisal Sox. The first thing that struck me was the size of the keys the guards—or, as they are now called, correctional officers—used to open and close doors and gates. As we passed through three gates, we went into a room to change clothes. I remember asking the officer assigned to our legion team if I could leave my billfold in the room and he said that would be all right because the door would be locked. Somehow those words, "door will be locked," stood in my mind for several years when finally it dawned on me that I was in a maximum security correctional facility—not a training school, not a reformatory, but a penitentiary. The officers in those days were equipped with loaded canes, which contained metal at the bottom of the cane. They did away with those armaments when they realized inmates could grab those canes and use them as weapons against the officers.

I remember the prison served us supper after the game in an upstairs dining room with trustees serving as waiters. I remember Selmer took my hat off during the meal telling me it wasn't appropriate when eating.

While in the dugout I heard inmates telling of their woes. One inmate I heard told about how he should have received a workhouse sentence instead of being in Stillwater. Another story I heard was how a player, who was convicted of sodomy, did not want his last name to be used in the scorebook because he came from a well-to-do family.

Many years ago, a Minneapolis dentist was convicted of killing one of his patients. His name was Arnold Axilrod and he was sentenced to serve time in Stillwater. It was a very high-profile trial, which was covered by Fox Channel 9's Harry Reasoner. Reasoner went on to become a reporter for 60 minutes on CBS, largely I believe because of his excellence in covering that long trial. On one of the trips to Stillwater, I inquired about Axilrod and was told he was working in the commissary. I never did see him in person.

One of my neighbors when I lived on the north side on Vincent Avenue was a princess of a lady named Yetta. She had a brother whom I had gotten to know at a pool hall I hung out at on Plymouth Avenue. He was crime prone and wound up killing a loan shark. The Minneapolis Police knew they had their man and arrested him and his partner. Yetta's brother was convicted and sentenced for I-don't-know-how-many years to Stillwater. The media quoted the arresting offices as saying they awoke him from a deep sleep. Imagine being able to sleep after committing a murder.

Before I had gotten to know Yetta's brother, I had my first encounter with the FBI. Seems they were looking for him and couldn't find him so this particular agent went around the block talking to Yetta's neighbors. I will never forget that day. It was around 6:00 p.m. when I heard a knock on the front door. Mom and I were eating supper and, when I went to answer, I saw a tall heavyset gentleman standing at the door. He didn't say anything, but pulled out his I.D. the size of a checkbook and showed it to me. I didn't see his picture or his name, just the signature of J. Edgar Hoover on it. I nearly fainted. In that moment I tried to think of what I had done that day. He then proceeded to tell me that he was looking for Yetta's brother and showed me a picture of him. I believe he also interviewed Mom. Two things about the FBI agent I will not forget: how immaculately he was dressed and the great length he went to say that it was no reflection of Yetta.

In subsequent summers, I saw Yetta's brother when we took our ball club up to Stillwater. We shook hands and I couldn't help noticing the look on his face. He looked very depressed. Prison life did not suit him at all. By the look on his face, he appeared to me to be remorseful. Some years later I read in the paper that he was granted a parole on the condition he get out and stay out of Minnesota. They reported that he went to make his home in Chicago where some years later I read in the Minneapolis paper that he passed away from natural causes. I have often wondered if it was a violent death, being that a person is known by the company he keeps, especially in a town Chicago's size.

Yetta's son Paul played first base for our legion team but I don't think he ever went to Stillwater when his uncle served time.

I met another friend of mine, Marvin Kramer at a softball game at North Commons in 1957. He had just been laid off at a prefabricated manufacturing company and eventually took a test for a clerk carrier at the Minneapolis Post Office. He passed it and became employed there. We hit it off right away. I will never forget the car he drove. It was a 1951 hardtop two-door Chevrolet with a white roof and yellow body. He was an excellent driver, which made me feel safe when we went to sporting events around town. He was a short 5' 2" tall and slightly overweight and was a heavy pipe smoker. When we both worked for our legion baseball club we were known as the M&M boys. This was when Mickey Mantle and Roger Maris were starring for the New York Yankees.

We attended many University of Minnesota baseball games together—first at the old Delta Field, and later on at the newly built Siebert Field next door. The most popular sportscaster at that time was Dick Nesbitt, who worked on Channel 5. He was a former Chicago Bears player. He was bald but had a big patch of hair on his forehead. He started out his telecast by saying, "You're looking great tonight."

On one particular Saturday, who should come to the game but Dick Nesbitt. He sat by himself and I don't think it took more than five minutes when a whole swarm of kids at Delta field came over to him. It was quite a tribute to a terrific guy. He passed away at the young age of 46.

In the area of Delta Field were railroad tracks that ran across left field. Students would get on the top of the train cars to watch games. Everything was okay until the cars started to move; the students started jumping off, but to the best of my knowledge, no one was hurt. What a sight it was. We watched two events: the ball game and students jumping off railroad cars.

Marvin later married and I began to lose contact with him in later years. He passed away some years ago at the young age of 54 from an apparent heart attack while shaving, getting ready to go to work that particular morning. It was a sad moment in my life to lose such a friend.

Another friend of mine was Glen Gostick, who coached our legion team in the late 50s to the early 60s. He would hold team meetings after the game was played, win or lose. The players were thoroughly disgusted with those meetings and showed their disgust by walking out of the meeting uttering some unsavory words. Glen was the Ph.D. of baseball. Together with Minnesota Gopher coach Dick Siebert, he co-authored the book *Playing Baseball*, which I had the privilege of reading many years ago. I was captivated not only by the written words on the fundamentals of the game, but also the pictorial content in it. I would highly recommend it for at least leisurely reading.

I once heard a friend of mine say that Glen was the best baseball player he had ever seen play the game at the high school and college level. Quite a tribute. Glen played pro baseball in the old New York Giant organization at the minor league level. Defensively, I was told, he had the mechanics, but the problem was he couldn't hit. That cost him a career in the big leagues.

I remember when Glen was the official scorer at a Minnesota Twins game. One of the Twins infielders made a play that Glen scored as an error, but Twins manager Tom

Kelly called it a hit. A heated argument ensued. Be that as it may, I will always back up Glen on any phase of the game.

I first met him during the high school baseball playoffs at the old Nicollet ballpark in 1952. What first caught my eye was the car he was driving. I don't remember what the make or year was, but it was a lot like Selmer's antique—a 1932 Chevrolet. At one time, I remember Glen giving me a ride home from the library in downtown Minneapolis when I ran into him over there. What caught my eye, as it was in the middle of the winter, was his catcher's mitt on the backseat of his car. When I expressed amazement, as it was wintertime, he said to me, "I never know when I will use it."

Glen had a friend by the name of Dick Cassidy, who was the kind of guy who would give someone the shirt off his back. Dick was also a great athlete who could have had a big-league career had it not been for a skiing accident. Dick was coaching the Camden legion team when he evidently begged Glen to sign a promising pitcher over to his Camden ball club. Glen caved in to his request. This particular pitcher attended a private Catholic school, but lived in our district. I remember Glen asking me my opinion on another pitcher, whom he was counting on to replace the promising pitcher, and while I told him I didn't like him, I wanted Glen to look at him to give him a chance as I did not want to stand in his way. I remember our athletic director shouting out "they're great buddies" when we were playing Dick's team. It was later on when a parent of one of the Camden players broke the news of this promising pitcher getting away from us. I was flabbergasted.

Glen always called me Scout, as I did some charting for him sitting in a chair behind home plate. In those days I used to go over to the University to watch the Gophers work out in the field house. I was watching a pitcher who was trying out for the team. Glen, who was an assistant coach in those days at the University, came over to where I was standing and shouted the greeting, "Hey Scout, how you doing?" This kid must have thought I was a big-league scout. Did he ever bear down. He probably thought I was going to sign him for a contract.

I ran into Glen a couple of years ago at a grocery store and asked him how things were going for him. He told me that he was umpiring and I asked him how he liked it. He told me "the team that wins thinks I did a good job and the team that loses thinks I did a horrible job."

Glen is a registered physical therapist. I don't know how much he practiced it but I do know he was a trainer for a pro hockey team in St. Paul at one time.

One of the most exciting and colorful people I was privileged to be associated with was the athletic director, Frank. I first met him at a legion ball game back in 1952 at the Northeast Athletic Field. It was an area that was occupied by Quonset huts, which served as temporary housing for returning veterans of World War II. It was a beautiful field kept up by the Minneapolis Park Board. I only wish North Commons Park was kept up that well. Frank's duties were mainly financial in nature, purchasing equipment like baseballs, uniforms, bats, etc. The legion would run bingo games at their hall to help finance their baseball program. They also sponsored a 4th of July carnival at North Commons. Frank was very frugal with money. One season, Glen took the club up to St. Cloud for an exhibition game. Coming home, Glen treated them to supper. When Glen turned in his expenses, Frank took him to task for spending too much. Frank never wanted to give the returning players new caps, saying they should wear their old ones.

The story goes that Frank got married in Preston, MN

on a Saturday morning and that afternoon he played baseball. When asked if it was true he replied "What else?"

Frank was a catcher in his playing days. I still remember Frank catching in a softball game at North Commons. He drove a 1948 four-door, two-tone blue Chevrolet. Frank had one brother, Bill, who was a star basketball player at North and was a Minneapolis fireman. One of his sons, Chuck, was afflicted with Down syndrome. I remember Bill taking Chuck to legion ball games and people would stare at him. What a feeling it must have been for Bill to be with Chuck at large gatherings of people.

Once at a Gopher baseball game a group of us were discussing an event going on in Burnsville, MN. Glen turned to Frank and jokingly asked him what the zip code of Burnsville was; Frank, who was a carrier for the Minneapolis Post Office, replied 55337, which was correct. Once, I ran into Frank driving his post office truck. I was looking for a company on his route. He told me to get in the back of the truck, covered me up with mail bags, and off we went directly to the location.

Firefighting was in Frank's blood. It seemed to have run in his family. As I stated earlier, Bill, his brother, was a Minneapolis fireman. Bill's son, Bill Jr., is a fire captain in a station in northeast Minneapolis, and Frank's grandfather was also a firefighter. The reason why Frank was not was because he could not stand heights. Occasionally Bill would talk about fires he was called to fight. There was a bad fire at a warehouse during that particular week. Frank, being interested in fires, spoke to Bill about that particular fire at a ball game. Bill said that the first responders found the fire extinguishers empty, which indicated to them that the employees had tried to put out the fire themselves before calling the fire department. It would have been a much less intense fire with much less loss of property and less danger to the firemen if they had been called in right away.

Once when I was helping Frank unload some fertilizer, he was in the house when the fire engines in a station house went out on a call about two blocks away. He stormed out of the house shouting, "Where did they go?" I replied that I didn't know and he shouted back to me, "You old so and so…sounds like they went up to Camden," an area in north Minneapolis. We went there in his car, but we couldn't find the engines and returned back to his home.

I will always think that Frank bought a home near a fire station to purposely keep a watch on their shifts.

Talking about baseball and firemen, the Fire and Police American Legion Post sponsored a team comprised mostly of baseball players from Edison High School in northeast Minneapolis. They would haul their players in a police paddy wagon. About three blocks from the park, they turned the lights and siren on.

One of my many disappointments over those 16 years of active involvement in the baseball program was that none of our players made it to the major leagues. I felt that Dick Naylor, Doug Gillen, Jack Rowles, all of whom played on Selmer's championship team in 1949, could have made it to the big league along with Joe Pollock, who was a pitcher who played for us from 1959-1961. He had a curve ball the likes I have never seen. He threw his arm out in a high school game and, even though he pitched at the U of M and won an NCAA World Series, he never regained his old form. I believe that the coach should have used him either in the outfield or at first base because he could hit, run, field, and throw with the best of them. But it wasn't to be. I saw him throw out a runner at home plate from the center field after he threw out his arm, an amazing feat. After college he signed to play for the old New York Giants but didn't advance up their minor league system. Last I heard, he was living in Denver.

The only player who did make it to the big leagues was Dave Thies, who attended Ascension grade school and Minneapolis De LaSalle, both Catholic schools. During the summer, he played for the Grain Exchange Post. While at Ascension he helped pitch Ascension to the Knights of Columbus City Championship. That team was coached by Bob Ball, a Minneapolis police detective who donated his off-duty time to Ascension and De LaSalle— not only in baseball, but in football, too.

As times passed, I became good friends with Bob Kammerer who played shortstop on that Ascension team.

3.

Health Care Providers

Back in 1946, Minneapolis had a severe outbreak of polio. Two of my neighbors' children passed away one after the other. During that time period, I began to have trouble swallowing. I soon got over it. But it started up again in the winter of 1957, while attending college. In June of that year, while taking a written exam, I later was to find that a panic attack had done me in. I felt I was going to faint. I started doing the exam coherently but halfway through, I scribbled through it. I got a C in the course only because of the instructor's generosity.

Ten years later, I took a course in social psychology from him. On the last day of class, all the students in the class of about 200 gave him a standing ovation. He was a gentleman and a scholar in the true sense of those words.

Previous to that I suffered my first panic attack while giving a speech in a communications class. I felt faint and had to sit down. Was I ever embarrassed. While I registered for classes in the fall of 1957, I found it necessary to cancel out. That was quite a blow to me. That winter I finally sought help. I saw a doctor and was told upon examination that I had fear of swallowing. He said if it was a fear I should be seen by a psychiatrist. I was referred to the University of Minnesota Hospitals.

In 1958, I voluntarily admitted myself to the U of M Station 60, an open-door unit with no bars on the windows as I was not perceived to be a danger either to myself or for those around me. I held the belief that electric shock could help me in overcoming my fear. When a group of us were playing volleyball on the roof, a resident psychiatrist came over to me and introduced himself. Dr. G was to become my psychiatrist during my five-week stay there and proved to me to be a nightmare. He repeatedly hounded me, asking questions I could not answer like why did my father suffer from an ulcer? How should I know? I repeatedly broke down, crying my heart out. He seemed to relish me crying.

I took many tests, such as the Minnesota Multiphasic personality. Dr. G did not pay close attention to the test results, so as I was to find out later on, he diagnosed me as being schizophrenic. Dr. G took me to a case conference and spilled the beans on me. At the case conference, a decision was made to teach me social skills and they prescribed Thorazine; they believed in those days it revolutionized state hospitals. One of the side effects of Thorazine is liver damage, so I repeatedly received blood tests. I still remember the medical technologist coming up to our floor to stick me with a needle. It reminded me of a carpenter's tool box.

Besides badgering me, Dr. G frequently used force on me, such as forcing me to eat supper when I was overwhelmed with fear. It was around 5:00 p.m. when I couldn't eat and went back to my room. Evidently the staff was alerted and Dr. G came in and forced me to the table, saying many times, "I'm going to insist that you do it my way."

Everything patients did was noted and doctors were told of what was said either to staff or amongst the other patients. In one instance, Dr. G came running in my room and said, "I heard you were talking about me." I did not deny it. I had mentioned that I thought he was a lousy doctor. Relations between us deteriorated by minute, hour, and day to the point where I felt I had to leave. Under my agreement with the University, I had to give three days written notice of my intention to leave. Sometime during that three-day period, he phoned my mother demanding that she commit me to a state hospital, telling her how sick I was and that they were not equipped to handle long-care patients. He never told me about his treatment plan, which I found out later was to teach me social skills. That along with Thorazine would supposedly cure my schizophrenia, as he envisioned it.

During my interviews, he kept telling me, "I want you to trust me. I want you to trust me." You have to earn trust and he did nothing to earn my trust. He never told me what his treatment plan was because he knew I wouldn't play ball with him. I was asked by the presiding doctor at a case conference what brought me to Station 60 and I told them point-blank it was fear. I never went to the hospital to learn social skills. I had no motivation to go in that direction. There is an old saying "You can lead a horse to water, but you can't make him drink." He never told me what the diagnosis was; I was to find out later.

Back in 1995, the media reported that Dr. G was under investigation by the FBI for possible Medicare and Medicaid fraud. It took 37 years, but I was finally vindicated. The real Dr. G was exposed.

After leaving Station 60, I sought the help of another doctor, Dr. L, whom I felt was not much better. I gave him my file from the University and he was the one who told me of Dr. G's diagnosis—schizophrenia. The file from Dr. G said I was looking for a magic cure. Dr. L also stated that I was looking for a magic cure. What a thing to say to a patient. Can you imagine a doctor in a branch of medicine accusing a patient of looking for a magic cure?

When I applied for social security disability, I was sent to see Dr. C, a staff psychiatrist at a Minneapolis hospital. He told me that he understood how difficult it was for me to work and he suggested I seek treatment at the hospital's day-treatment program, which I later did. In Dr. C's report to social security, which I was able to read, he diagnosed me as suffering from latent schizophrenia and said that with drugs I would be helped. He never mentioned what drugs would, in his opinion, help me.

In the beginning of his interview with me, he noted that he thought I would decompensate, whatever that means. I told him that the social security disability decision contained many flaws. He asked me how I would run it and told him it should be run on a case conference attended by (1) the examining physician, (2) a social worker (in my case, a psychiatric social worker at the masters level), (3) an attorney schooled in social security law, (4) a registered nurse with experience working in a mental health unit either inpatient or outpatient, and (5) possibly an occupational therapist working in that specialized area. He said that made sense.

Dr G told me that my I.Q. was between 120-130. After two years on disability, I became eligible for Medicare. They again sent me to see Dr. C and I remember him saying to me, "Mr. Friedell, are you mad?" This happened when Ronald Reagan was president and publically said he was going to save social security from insolvency by targeting the disabled. Talk about compassion. Dr. C asked me if it was right to people paying into the system and having people like me be a beneficiary. I told him I never would have applied if I was able to work. I'm not one who cheats the government. I also asked him if it was fair to pay into the system to protect people who become disabled and then deny them benefits that are legally theirs.

After my initial application was turned down for a second time, I appealed that decision to the Bureau of Hearings and Appeals of the Social Security Administration. Because of a large backlog of hearings, they brought in an administrative law judge and his secretary from Fort Worth, TX. Taxpayers paid for expenses such as travel, hotel lodging, etc. The decision to deny my claim was made by a foreign doctor—a psychiatrist who could not be licensed to practice in America, but could work for the government. He said that I did not meet or equal the listings as set down by the Secretary of Human Services.

During my 24 years on disability I was red-flagged a couple of times. One of those times I was examined by a psychiatrist in private practice. During the exam, he appeared to be unconcerned; I think he felt that I should not be receiving that entitlement. This was reinforced when he did not send in the results of the exam. After two months, I asked what the agency could do to help me. They said they had contacted him twice and he did not respond. The only thing was for them to withhold payment. Apparently that didn't bother him, so I decided to take matters in my own hands by going up to his office and telling his receptionist I was not going to leave until the report was in the mail. She told me that it takes time and it wouldn't get into the mail until the next day, so I left.

One of the psychiatrists the Social Security Administration wanted to examine me was someone that I grew up with. I told my disability staffer to send me to another doctor to complete the review. Turns out it worked in my favor. A local news station investigated the person I grew up with, who also examined recruits wanting to go into the military. He was rejecting them as unfit to serve. Parents complained and the news station found that, with one exception, all those in question on further examination were found mentally competent to serve in the military. The news station found that the doctor felt these recruits would claim disability so they would draw service-connected payments from the government. The doctor, as a result, lost his license to practice in Minnesota and the last I heard was working in a state hospital in Colorado.

Between seeing Dr. C and going to the day treatment center, I saw Dr. S, a staff psychiatrist at a local hospital. He was constantly being disciplined for his erratic behavior. He prescribed Navane along with Cogentin. One of the side effects of Navane is tardive dyskinesia, a neurological disorder which causes shaking. So that's why I took Cogentin.

I attended the day-treatment program for awhile and I noticed immediately how times changed. I was treated with dignity and respect by the entire staff. The Chief of the service was Dr. J, who was present at my case conference at the University, where he was a resident psychiatrist. During the time period when I left the University and entered the day-treatment program, he came to the conclusion that push-pull did not necessarily result in click-click. The resident in charge was Dr. P, who treated the entire patient load in a high-class, high-caliber fashion.

After leaving the day-treatment program, I was seen by another doctor who continued to prescribe Navane. I left that doctor in 1981 after being taken off that drug; he told me, "I think you can do it." The day I left, I promised myself that I would never seek treatment for mental illness again. I felt I could get better advice at my friendly neighborhood barbershop for the price of a haircut.

During my review with Social Security, I was sent to see Dr. K, a psychiatrist in private practice in Minneapolis. Finally, a psychiatrist who could spell compassion with a capital "C" instead of a small "c." I was in a state of shock when he told me he would put in a good word for me and if I was denied, he encouraged me to appeal it immediately. He was on my side—imagine that! Among other things, he said I was barely existing. I envy people like that. What an asset they are to the community.

As years went by, I began being treated for hypertension. During those years I was being treated by Dr. E, an internist. Dr. E came highly recommended and I was told he finished second in his class in medical school. That was good enough for me. He helped me for 15 years until he retired. He gave me 15 years of life without damage to the kidneys, heart, or brain. Quite a feat considering the person I am. However, I remember one time him telling me I should go to work, that I would feel better having a sense of accomplishment as much as he did. It actually resulted in a shouting match. He also told me I was cheating the government, and when I told him I was seeing a psychiatrist, he told me, "I didn't think you had it in you." As I saw it as a sign of weakness, he saw it as a sign of strength.

Through the years I have been seen by many doctors whose professional expertise has enabled me to keep fighting for a better day. Several stand out in my mind: Dr. Michael Kelly, a family practitioner; Dr. Kurt Demel, a hematologist-oncologist, whom I see for colon cancer; and Dr. Heefner, a psychiatrist.

What distinguishes these doctors is the way they relate to their patients; they both have mild-mannered attitudes. I look at them as more than doctors; I look at them as close friends.

Dr. Kelly told me his brother died from Hodgkin's disease in his early 30s. What a tragedy, especially for a doctor standing by helplessly.

After Dr. Kelly's clinic closed, I started seeing Dr. Gayl Gustafson, a family practitioner. On one of my visits, she suggested that I have a colonoscopy. It turned out she saved my life as I was diagnosed as having colon cancer. The surgeon told me that the prognosis is good. That made me happy. So far I weathered the storm.

The only bad experience I had outside of psychiatry was with an urologist. I was scheduled for a biopsy of the prostate. I took an antibiotic pill; one tablet cost me $40. I called Metro Mobility to schedule a round trip from where I live to the clinic. After prepping and taking the antibiotic, I showed up in time for the procedure. When I signed in, I was told that the doctor had surgery scheduled at the same time. I was beside myself. How could he schedule two procedures at the same time?

That surgery was not an emergency as he showed up about half an hour later to do the biopsy. Evidently he was called and told how upset I was. Thank goodness the biopsy showed no cancer.

After we sold our house on the north side, we moved to St. Louis Park where I frequented a White Castle in the morning and Knollwood Mall. As time passed at the Castle, I became friends with a large group who discussed the affairs of the world. When one person in the group passed on, we went to his funeral, that's how close we were. At Knollwood, there was an older group who also discussed the affairs of the world. I said very little during those get-togethers because I felt much younger than the others. I just listened. During my years on the street, I was daily overcome with panic attacks—and boredom. I could not control it. As far as fear was concerned, I could avoid being in situations where fear would engulf me. Not so with swallowing. Somehow, some way, I managed to eat, but at times it was difficult at best. I thought that schizophrenia was the cause and I would have to live the rest of my life with fear. How wrong I was.

In April of 1991, an article appeared in the *Minneapolis Star Tribune* on the front page that a new drug had been found for schizophrenia. I was elated. I saw Dr. E and he encouraged me to go for it.

My insurance led me to see a new psychiatrist, Dr. Heefner, who, when I told him of the diagnosis, felt I was not schizophrenic, but he wanted to await the results of the Multiphasic. The results proved him right. I was not schizo, but suffered from depression causing panic attacks. I told him I had been prescribed Navane and he said he could not understand why. On my second visit, he told me he was still trying to understand why I was given Navane. He told me that the anti-depressant Imipramine might help, but he emphatically stated it was not a promise. I told him that I found out about it 33 years ago. It turned out that it helped me from getting panic attacks. Imipramine has been out in the market since 1958, the year I voluntarily signed myself in Station 60 at the University Hospital.

This is what really hurts. All those years, living with a diagnosis of schizophrenia and being a street person, passed me by. What a terrible thing to do to a patient.

I continued to see Dr. Heefner for several years until he retired, saying it was time to move on. He told me that day that he was being treated for prostate cancer and he had bypass surgery. He is a brilliant scholar as evidenced by his being a member of Phi Beta Kappa at Iowa State University where he did his undergraduate work.

4.

Family

As my life was filled with a misdiagnosis of schizophrenia and drugs that did not help me, I watched the lives of those around me unfold. As my life passed me by, I watched their successes and their losses.

I've already mentioned my Uncle Max and Aunt Clara. They were strange people who I believe could not face reality. Uncle Max simply did not want to work; work was not in Aunt Clara's vocabulary. She was brought up by my grandparents as a weakling and made the most of it. Mom said that she was a music teacher in Russia, teaching piano. Unfortunately, she never mastered the English language and I still remember Mom writing to her in Russian whenever she wanted to communicate with her.

Aunt Clara was very thin—less than 100 pounds, I'm sure. Whether she suffered from anorexia nervosa, I do not know. I saw her put food in her purse to pretend to others that she was cleaning her plate at a reception here in Minneapolis many years ago.

Both Aunt Clara and Uncle Max had neat gimmicks up their sleeves. As one of their former neighbors told me, she doesn't know how they made it. Whether they lived on welfare, I will never know, but I do know that Uncle Max played bingo to try to make ends meet and get rich quick. Unfortunately, that never happened and whenever they needed money to survive, Uncle Max tooted his horn and

Mom responded immediately, sending them her entire paycheck.

When I talked to Mom about it, she lied to me and said she sent small gifts to them because, as she put it, they were starving. Later on in a telephone conversation I heard her say that she sent her whole payroll checks to them.

My mother did a lot for them and their kids did nothing for her. They could have called her up to check on how things were going for her, taking her out to lunch, going to the movies, taking her to the beauty shop, or making sure she kept doctor and dentist appointments. I assumed they were ashamed in the way their parents acted. They should have been! I will never understand how parents can bring up their family of three children and not want to work to support them. It is an act of criminality to permit such actions by parents, and my mother played right into their hands. I will never forgive them for their actions.

The fact that they could come to my mom for help and I, her son, could not, was a big factor for being on the street for 33 years watching traffic—both pedestrian and vehicular.

Another of my mother's sister was Aunt Sadie. One thing I will say about Aunt Sadie was that, in all my years, I've never known anybody with such a high work ethic. She never told anybody where she worked, but work she did. She was a widow, losing two husbands: one during the flu epidemic in 1918; and another from a ruptured appendix. She had two children, Anne and Daniel.

Daniel was married to Ruth and had several children. Their son Jonathon and his wife Ebby have three children—one of them, Tova, recently got married in New York.

Daniel and Ruth's son, Sherman, married a Russian immigrant, Natasha. They have two children: a daughter Paulina and a son Andrew. I attended Paulina's bat mitzvah at the Temple of Aaron in St. Paul and was amazed at how well she did. She conducted the entire service all by herself—an amazing feat. From the beginning to the end, through it all she did it in the spirit of Judaism. She is currently an honor student. Sherman and Natasha have a bumper sticker on their car that reads "Proud Parents of an Honor Student." She also plays the flute in the school's band in Eagan.

Their son Andrew is very handsome looking and plays a wicked game of chess, mainly with his grandfather, Misha. I am looking forward to attending his bar mitzvah and seeing him do the same job as his sister Paulina. What a treat that will be. Sherman's in-laws immigrated to America with Natasha's mom's parents. Her grandfather recently passed away but, as far as I know her grandmother is still living. They came to America to realize the American dream and they sure found it, especially in their grandchildren Paulina and Andrew.

Daniel and Ruth's son Zachary is employed at a publishing company as an artist. He is a very creative individual and has taught at the Loft Literary Center. He was married to Polly. It was an interfaith faith marriage in which a divorce is pending. They have two children, Kara and David. Kara is a brilliant student and is captain of the cheerleaders at her high school. She is planning to go to college and has applied for a cheerleader's scholarship at the University of Hawaii. I wish her well in all her future endeavors. She deserves it.

Zachary and Polly's son David is autistic. I have seen him on several occasions and he seems to be out of control. Still he does attend public school in a children-with-special-needs program. I don't know if he will be bar mitzvahed when he turns 13.

Daniel and Ruth's son Michael is married to Ellen and has two sons, Josh and Noah. Josh is a PhD candidate at the University of Minnesota in, I believe, pharmaceutical chemistry. I always wanted a PhD relation on my mother's side of the family and finally, my dreams have come true. To top it off, he is a super kid. Brains and character go together.

Their other son Noah is a business major at the University of Minnesota's Carlson School of Management. I don't know what his major field of interest in business is, but whatever field it is, I'm sure he will be successful. That's just the kind of person he is.

I have met Ellen's parents and they are high-class, high-character individuals. They have been very good to Mom. When Noah was bar mitzvahed, they honored Mom by calling her up to the Torah—an event I will never forget.

The last of Ruth and Daniel's children is their only daughter, who is not married and is in her late thirties or early forties. She is employed as an administrative assistant and seems to be enjoying her job. Some time ago she moved out of the house and bought a home in Minneapolis near the north side in a crime-ridden area. She has two dogs to keep her company. She is still single.

Daniel died at the young age of 41 of some form of bone cancer. He left five children all under the age of thirteen. He did not live to even see his children become bar mitzvahed or bat mitzvahed. Some people I have come to know over the years have been cheated in life, others out of life. Daniel was cheated out of life. What a tragedy. He served in the Army during World War II. I remember writing to him during that time and he always answered me back. I believe the letters he sent me were called V8 mail and appeared to be censored. It appeared on duplicate paper. I once asked LeEtta, his daughter, if she remembers her father and while she still remembers her grandmother Sadie, she doesn't remember him.

Ruth has remarried to Abe Goldberg: a fine gentleman whom she met at a singles gathering at a community center. She seems to be very happy and I am happy for her. She's had a bout of cancer at a young age and made a wonderful recovery. I understand she goes for yearly check-ups at the Mayo Clinic.

Aunt Sadie's other child was daughter Anne who was married to Max, a holocaust survivor. They have two children: a daughter Brendal, who is an optometrist; and Sammy, who is both a registered pharmacist and a podiatrist working out of his home. Anne, Brendal, and Sammy all live in Brooklyn. I visited them when I went there to attend Sammy's daughter's bat mitzvah.

Brendal is married to David, who is an accountant for the State of New York, working in New York City. Brendal has two children. From what I understand Brendal practices two days a week at a Veterans hospital on Long Island. She is a very intelligent lady. Before she got married she practiced privately, doing teaching and research and presenting papers nationally.

My grandparents owned a duplex at 1010 Fremont and left no will when they passed, so their duplex was up for grabs. Aunt Sadie, who was renting a home with her two kids, offered to take care of my grandmother when grandfather passed away if she obtained the duplex. So who did she go to but Mom. This is another example of a relation who went to Mom, for my way of thinking, for selfish reasons. This is another example of Mom listening to others and not giving me a chance to talk to her. Mom always said it was Uncle Ben who should have gotten title to the duplex. Aunt Sadie promised to take care of my grandmother in return for not having to go into a nursing home.

Speaking from my personal experience it is an impossible task to take care of an elderly parent while being saddled down in a full-time job. Mom never forgave Aunt Sadie for the shabby way she treated grandmother, but she consoled herself in that grandmother did not have to go into a nursing home. In my opinion, the residence should have been sold and money received used to pay her bill at the nursing home.

All Aunt Sadie wanted was the money from the property, which she got when the city tore it down. There was a lien on the house and Aunt Sadie was extremely concerned about how much she would get. She loved money, was willing to work for it, but I will always believe the sale of the property was distributed inappropriately. Mom also said what weighed heavily in her decision was Aunt Sadie's help to get the family settled in America. She told the story of when Aunt Sadie preceded the rest of the family in coming over and how she stayed at another aunt's apartment.

Sadie could not speak a word of English and still was able to obtain employment. Her aunt tried to help her out by making sure she knew the address where they lived. The apartment had a "for rent" sign on the front lawn. Her aunt told her what that sign said in English—"For Rent"—and that she lived in "For Rent." Confident that she was starting to master the English language, she went to work. What she didn't realize was that during the course of the day, the landlord rented out the apartment and took down the sign. While at work, Sadie became friendly with a coworker who also spoke Russian. At the end of the day Aunt Sadie walked home with her friend and, much to her astonishment, could not find an apartment with a "For Rent" sign. So Sadie went to her friend's apartment, called her aunt who then took her home. Such was the lot of the Russian immigrant in 1921—a far cry from what it is today.

Aunt Sadie had the first television in the family. It was a 12" Admiral. We would go over to her house on Friday nights to watch TV.

My mother's brother was Uncle Ben Tutelman. He was an outstanding meat cutter and worked in several butcher shops before marrying, and then went to work at Swift Packing Co. in South St. Paul. He married late in life to a woman named Esther. There is an interesting story on how the two met. Aunt Sadie wanted him to get married off and said she knew a peddler who had a daughter who was single. It ended with them getting married. His marriage to her was a huge mistake, in the way she treated him throughout their marriage; she completely dominated him. I remember when they were both at our house and someone said a good fortune struck them; she must have run about five yards to knock on wood—a tree. One of her brothers was named Nathan, who was married to a lady named Marcella. When my sister got married there was a big argument whether they would be invited. Aunt Esther demanded they be invited and eventually they were. I remember how they danced together at my sister's wedding. They seemed to be madly in love. Tragically, Marcella passed away shortly after at a young age.

A sister of Esther's was married and had two sons: Marve, who is an accountant and Len, who last I heard was doing consulting work in St. Paul.

Len was an outstanding track star at Humboldt High School in St. Paul and at the University of Minnesota, where he majored in Education. He taught for a while in the St. Paul school district and decided to go into politics. He ran for a seat on the St. Paul City Council and was elected fourth-ward alderman. When Rudy Perpich became governor of Minnesota, he selected Len to be his Commissioner of Human Services, even though Len had no background in the social service area. Len later became Commissioner of the Department of Transportation even though he had no background in Civil engineering, all because he was a vocal supporter of Governor Perpich. After Perpich was defeated, Len went into consulting work. He was an educator who didn't understand that politics is a cause, not a career.

Another brother of Aunt Esther's was a Swift Packing Co. manager who got Uncle Ben hazardous tasks, which injured him quite often. I remember Mom often complaining about the hazardous jobs to which he was assigned, just so Aunt Esther would have more money in the household. Uncle Ben was a kind soul, not too intelligent, and he wouldn't harm a fly. I heard Aunt Esther deluged him with food and demanded he eat it all up. When I saw him at my sister's wedding, he looked very overweight. I believe, among his aliments, he had diabetes, which could have been caused by his obesity.

I remember Mom telling me how much he adored me as a child.

When Uncle Ben died, Aunt Esther called and said that she couldn't afford to pay the final expenses. I will always believe that this was a shakedown for the way the sale of the duplex was handled, because Uncle Ben should have gotten money.

The next maternal relation I want to write about is Aunt Rebecca, who was married to David and had two sons, Harry and Yale. Harry was married to Leona, whom we called Lee, and they had two adopted children, Robin, who was named after Aunt Rebecca, and a son Barry who was named after Uncle Ben. Yale was married to Diane, a convert, and they had two daughters Vicky and Judy. Judy, the eldest, was named after my grandfather Joseph, but I don't know who Vicky was named after.

Yale had a tragic life losing Diane to brain cancer at only age 38 and, shortly after that, losing Vicky at age 16 because of cancer of the pituitary gland. What a tragedy. I attended Diane's services and I remember Vicky crying at the graveside of her mom. I couldn't bring myself to attend Vicky's services.

My cousin Judy got Yale together with Eve Lynn Miller, who is affectionately called Cookie, and after a short courtship they were married at the Adath Jeshuran Synagogue in an elaborate ceremony officiated by Rabbi Arnold Goodman, which I attended. The reception was held at the Radisson South in Bloomington and what a feed it was. I remember a chef carving up a large salmon. I will never forget that scene. Before Yale marched down the aisle, he went in a room and cried his heart out. Could you blame him after losing both Vicky and Diane, both at such a young age? He was later to tell my mother that not a day went by that he didn't cry. What a loss.

The best way to describe Uncle Dave was laziness. Give him a bed to sleep in, chicken for a meal, and Aunt Rebecca to wait on him hand and foot, and he would be content. He was a furrier who lost his job when his boss's wife complained that Aunt Rebecca wore nicer clothes than she did. After losing his job as a furrier, he went to work at the Northside Bakery on Plymouth Avenue in Minneapolis. He was a member of a Teamsters Union and received union benefits, which included medical insurance. But being the type of person he was, LAZY, he decided to leave the job at the bakery with the benefits to open up his own grocery store on Golden Valley Road. It was called Karsh's Grocery Store and Delicatessen with, of course, Aunt Rebecca at his side constantly. Their home was close by so he took advantage of the short distance to frequently go home and nap. Mom would always say that Aunt Rebecca would have to scrub the floors at the store when Uncle Dave took nap breaks. He just refused to do it. There were rumors of them selling beer to minors and I remember Mom asking me if she should pass those rumors to Aunt Rebecca; I advised her to keep quiet which, I believe she did. In my opinion, it is a terrible way to do business knowing you are violating the law especially if it involves underage drinking. The newscasts are constantly filled with news about drivers being under the influence of alcohol. I've seen horrific pictures of car crashes sometimes involving death. If one of his underage customers who he sold beer to would have been involved, what a terrible conscience he would have for the rest of his life—if he had a conscience at all.

Uncle Dave was a stutterer of a high magnitude who never seemed to try to get help for his impediment. Mom used to say that only Aunt Rebecca could understand him. He was also a chain smoker. The one good thing I could say about him was that he was a very good father. He understood the job of being a father to Yale and Harry, considering he lost his father at an early age.

Harry was working as a manager in Rapid City, South

Dakota when he married. Uncle Dave went down to Rapid City and brought him back to Minneapolis for his wedding. Uncle Dave knew, considering that Harry was an extremely nervous person (and may have had some neurological condition), that it would be emotionally hard on him to drive all that distance. When my father passed, it was Uncle Dave who broke the news to Harry and not Aunt Rebecca. Uncle Dave was also good to Yale. I can only guess that it was in his makeup. I only wish my father possessed those attributes. Had my parents possessed those attributes, I never would have been a street person for 33 years. I'm convinced of that.

When Uncle Dave left his job at the bakery, he also lost his medical insurance. When Aunt Rebecca was diagnosed with multiple myeloma, cancer of the bone, which is treatable but not curable, the family had no insurance to cover her treatment. At that time, the old Mount Sinai Hospital had a free-bed fund, which Uncle Dave and Aunt Rebecca were forced to accept. I can only image the loss of dignity, self-esteem, and respect they suffered when she was diagnosed with that fatal disorder. Because of Dave's laziness, he couldn't have cared less of what the future might hold for him. Just give him a bed to sleep on, a chicken to eat, and, as my dad would call her, a "servant" to tend to business, and Dave was in his glory. I still remember him telling my mother when Dad passed that wives did not take care of their husbands. What a way to console a grieving widow on the very same day this tragedy occurred.

When Aunt Rebecca got sick, her son Harry was working in Rapid City, so that left the job of caring for her entirely up to Yale since Uncle Dave had trouble communicating because of his speech impediment. The doctor was up front with the family and told them it was fatal. Yale decided not to break the news to Aunt Rebecca, but instead told her she had a cold in her legs. When my mother constantly asked him of Rebecca's condition, Yale finally broke down and told her the truth, saying he just didn't have the heart to tell her of her pending demise.

I could never figure cousin Yale out. Aunt Rebecca was constantly raving about him and Harry. When Yale passed his driving test, Mom never heard the end of how he rode along with a policeman who actually worked for the State of Minnesota as a driver examiner. Rebecca constantly bragged about him taking a typing class in order to do his job as an insurance investigator. She bragged so loud that I assume he must have passed the course. That's what type of mother she was. Her kids would not have been so successful had it not been for their parents being there for them—and they were. If only my parents were like that, I too would have become a contributing member of society. I will always believe that.

Aunt Rebecca was overcome by hate at anyone she felt interfered in the world of her kids, Yale and Harry.

I was a college freshman enrolled in the general college when my dad passed on. General college was considered a college for underachieving students. Cousin Yale was also enrolled in that college. Aunt Rebecca made a Shiva call, along with Rabbi Nahum Schulman, who was also there. When the Rabbi who delivered the eulogy asked me what college I was enrolled in, I noticed a look on Aunt Rebecca's face—she appeared full of glee that I was an underachieving student. They say that a look on a person's face can mean a thousand words. On her face it meant two thousand words. She was my aunt and I was her nephew and still, in a tragic moment in my life, she hated me.

In 1946, Redl & Redlich did a study in Detroit of "Children Who Hate." The two child psychiatrists concluded that children who had the trait of hatred were brought up in a very strict environment.

I think my maternal grandfather, Joseph Tutelman, was a strict disciplinarian who believed that children should be seen and not heard. It seemed to affect Aunt Rebecca to a great extent. I will always feel that when she passed, anger and hate did her in, and not multiple myeloma.

Mom would tell the story of how Aunt Rebecca was fearful of mice. When the family left Russia they hid out in a farmer's house during the day as Russia did not permit people to emigrate. So the story goes that the farmer who hid them out had a son named Mishka who was always in trouble with the police. Mish in Russian means a mouse, and when the police came looking for him and asked for Mishka, she mistakenly thought they were looking for mice. She almost blew their cover.

I believe Aunt Rebecca was a terrible influence on Mom. Aunt Rebecca was taller than Mom and Mom was scared of her. Mom told me that before Rebecca passed on, she asked Mom who she should give her diamond ring to—Yale or Harry. I don't know to this day what Mom told her.

Harry passed away about six years ago from multiple myeloma at, I believe, age 68. For some reason I always felt sorry for him. It appeared to me that he felt he was an underdog in every venture he went into. I once told him when he was selling cars for a small dealership he'd better himself by going to work for a larger dealership. He told me how he felt that he was not ready to make that move. One thing he was good at was sales.

I never had much contact with both Yale and Harry after Aunt Rebecca passed, but when I last saw Harry at my cousin Johnny's funeral, he told me he was in the insurance business and one of his clients was The American

Federation of State, County, and Municipal Employees (AFSCME), of which I was a member when I worked for the State.

Harry and Yale never got along and didn't speak to each other for a long period of time. I understand Yale went to visit Harry in the hospital when he was in his final hours. I wish I was there to hear their last words. It must have been quite a scene.

Mom always bemoaned the fact that they disliked each other and I told her that is what happens when you grow up in a sea of hate. Yale and Harry never thought much of each other. Yale wasn't the smartest of my cousins. He flunked one grade and spent some time in what was called a "special class." I heard that Harry told him to do very poorly on an intelligence test so he wouldn't have to work to achieve a normal sense of scholarship. Yale followed his advice and wound up in a special class. Still Rebecca felt he was Phi Beta Kappa material—a superstar.

I remember the both of us playing catch with a baseball at a street in front of his house. The house was located on a hill and Yale stood on the upside of the hill and I on the lower side, so if I overthrew him, he would not have to run far to retrieve it, while if he overthrew the ball, it would go downhill and I would have to go a long distance to retrieve it. Yale must have taken baseball seriously as he was practicing throwing the ball around and broke a window in the house. He was left-handed, as am I, and was a pretty good player but never pursued it further than the sandlot.

I remember having stomach trouble and Mom told Aunt Rebecca. I believe Aunt Rebecca told Yale because I remember Yale and a bunch of his friends—he had a lot of them—pointing their fingers at me and yelling at me while I walked down the street. I can only surmise that Aunt Rebecca had a field day bad-mouthing me. That's the kind of person she was and my parents turned their backs on me. She always blamed Yale's friends for his inter-faith marriage and not herself or Uncle Dave. My mom would say Aunt Rebecca had a heart of gold and in return would say what heart. She had a heart of cast iron and not a heart of gold. A woman of valor she was not.

The next aunt I want to mention is Aunt Polly who was married to Phillip Krasner. He, among other ventures, was involved in moonshining. Under the Volstead Act, liquor was a forbidden commodity in the 1920s and 30s. However, that didn't keep people like Uncle Phillip from producing it under the cover of darkness. Hence they were called moonshiners. I believe the sentences handed out for such an offense were one year and one day in the workhouse. Because Phillip did serve time for moonshining, their oldest son Leo was forced to drop out of school and work as a truck driver for the City of Minneapolis. What made matters worse was that this occurred during the depression of the 1930s.

The Krasner's were very family-oriented. Polly and Phillip's children helped my mother reach the tender age of 100 and are currently helping me through my various ailments and just plain existing. I'm always invited to holiday doings and they've even offered to take me grocery shopping at various times. For this, I am thankful and try to show my appreciation by inviting them to a family supper at Knollwood Place's dining room on a Friday night and a kiddush after Saturday morning services at Kenesseth Israel Synagogue, an orthodox synagogue in St. Louis Park, MN. A kiddush basically consists of refreshments served after the services. It's a tasty event that includes various delicacies. For all the things my parents did for the relations, Aunt Polly and Uncle Phillip's family did the most for Mom and me. They never asked for anything in return. The other relations would never call Mom up to ask how she was getting along, take her to the beauty shop, have coffee with her, or invite her to have lunch. They couldn't have cared less. My feeling was they were ashamed of how their parents acted toward my parents; they felt my parents were vulnerable. I have often said that my cousins should not be blamed for my being on the street watching traffic. The Krasners were just the opposite. They even have a "Krasner Club," which occasionally has reunions. After Mom passed away, I told them there will never be enough thank-yous to go around—and what more could my sister and I ask?

Uncle Phillip and Aunt Polly had four children: Leo, Florence, Rose, and Shirley. Leo has since passed and was married to Shirley Ravitz of St. Paul. They have two children: Judy who is married to Ross, an insurance executive, since retired; and Steve, who is married to Faye, and they have one daughter, Joanna, living in Chicago, IL and working for the federal government in a social services capacity.

Steve and Faye are the proud grandparents of a girl born to their daughter, Joanna.

Judy and Ross are parents of two children, Natalie and Jay. Natalie is living with her boyfriend, Steve. They've lived together for the past 18 years. Steve converted to Judaism and is a pleasant fellow whose mother I have met on several occasions. Jay is married and has two children: Leo, who is autistic and seems to be doing great; and Karen. Jay is married to Nancy, who is Catholic and refused to convert. They are raising their children in the Jewish faith and attend services at the Bethel Synagogue. I believe Karen is attending preschool at Bethel. Jay is in the insurance business much like his father and seems to be doing fine. They live in South Minneapolis. Leo attends the neighborhood school in the district and occasionally needs the assistance of a teacher's aide. Nancy is a registered nurse and works weekends at an urgent-care clinic.

Aunt Polly's daughter, Florence, is married to Jules. She was a war bride back in 1942. Jules was a junk peddler who made a handsome living. They lived in a beautiful home, which my mother and I visited quite often. Florence was a masterful chef whose cooking I very much enjoyed.

There's a story in the family that Aunt Sadie, who at that time lived in South St. Paul, was visiting Aunt Polly in North Minneapolis. Aunt Sadie adored baby Florence and decided to take her to her home to South St. Paul. When Aunt Polly couldn't find her, she immediately suspected that Sadie had kidnapped her. She found Sadie and Florence soon thereafter safe and sound.

Jules and Florence have four children. Ellen, who was married to Manny, and I believe has three kids and resides in Skokie, IL. Gary, who I think is divorced and is working in Chicago in some sort of legalized gambling. Dennis, who later changed his name to Modehai Hershtein when he became involved in the ultra-orthodox movement, and has, I believe, three kids.

Modehai has been married three times. I have met all three of his wives at one time or another. His ex-wife Hannah also changed her first name. I got to know her pretty well. She was divorced from her first husband.

I attended Modehai and Hannah's wedding and thoroughly enjoyed myself. I was deeply saddened when I heard they were divorcing. Modehai is currently working out of his apartment as a handyman. I don't know how successful his business has been. I got to know him pretty well when he started coming to services at Kenesseth Israel on Saturday mornings.

Jules and Florence's fourth child is Paul. Paul has been

on a troubled path and has served time at Lino Lakes Correctional Facility. One Saturday morning last summer when I was taking the bus to services, Paul got on the bus and recognized me. We talked for a couple of minutes and he told me that he stayed overnight at his mother's apartment and was headed to work, which I later found out was not true.

The next of Aunt Polly's children is Shirley, whose husband's name is Harold. Harold was a traveling furniture salesman along with his father Bill. I believe they ran a successful business. Shirley and Harold have four daughters. Marcia, who is married to Bruce Campbell, a convert. Andrea who is married. Patty is divorced, only having been married for six months in an interfaith marriage. The last of Shirley and Harold's daughters is Renee, who was married to Tony, and I believe they have two daughters. I've seen Renee at family gatherings with a male companion. Whether she is married to him remains a mystery to me. Marcia and Bruce have no children, the same for Patty.

Andrea and her husband have two sons, one of whom is a redhead with a beautiful head of hair, something like a bald-headed man like me would like to have.

Shirley and Harold currently reside in West St. Paul, MN.

The last of Aunt Polly's children is Rose Kay, whom I can only describe as having a heart of gold. She was married to a furniture salesman named Harold, but their marriage ended in a divorce. Harold and Rose together had one daughter, Sandi, who is married to a salesman named Jeff. Sandi and Florence were the only cousins who cried when I broke the news of mother's death to them over the phone. Sandi and Jeff have two children, Michelle and Adam. Michelle is married to Steve and they have two children, daughter Jonna and son Noah.

Their son Adam is a server in a restaurant in Minneapolis. He is not married. He attended a technical school but could not find a job after graduation in that field so he went back to serving.

Of all my cousins' spouses, I like Steve the most. We hit it off right away. At a gathering I told him I did not like the produce at a local grocery store. He told me in a mild manner that he disagreed with me. He didn't ridicule, shame me in front of others, or otherwise find fault with me in front of others. That's the kind of guy he is.

Steve and Michelle met through a Jewish dating service in Minneapolis. I am happy for the both of them.

Rose remarried to a fellow named Johnny of Winnipeg, Canada. Johnny and Rose had two sons, Phillip and Joey. I think that Phillip has been married several times while Joey has never married. Both of them currently reside in Florida. Both have steady jobs. Rose spends the winters in Florida and calls to see how I'm getting along, of which I am very appreciative.

Rose and Johnny also have a daughter Pam, who is married to Jerry Lehman. They have two children: Polly, who is named after Aunt Polly; and a son Lee. Polly will be Bat Mitzvahed soon. Pam works at an HMO and Jerry seems to go from job to job. When I am with them, I enjoy their company in that it is easy to communicate with them.

Rose and Johnny helped Mom quite a bit. One time that I will never forget is when Mom got an infection in her right hand. As I do not have a car, Mom called Rose and Johnny to take her to Urgent Care because she was also running a fever. They immediately took her to Urgent Care and then immediately to Abbot Northwestern Hospital for inpatient care. That caring attitude saved my mother from a possible amputation. There will never be enough thank-yous to go around.

One thing I have admired about Rose is that she speaks her mind. I respect her for that gift. When I had my hip surgery, the surgeon asked me as I prepared to go into surgery if I had anybody I wanted him to talk to and I said no. After the procedure I was put in the recovery room and then to my room at North Memorial Medical Center. Shortly after that who should walk in but Rose. I was overcome with joy upon seeing her. She told me that she had talked to the doctor and the surgery was successful. She visited me quite often during both surgeries—hip and colon—not only in the hospitals but in the nursing home as well. She and Ruth were present during my colon surgery, coming all the way from Minneapolis to St. Paul's Regions Hospital. Knowing that I had cousins like that—those who cared—made my recovery complete.

Dad's Side of the Family

My dad's sister Clara was married to Nathan Sherman and had three children, Morris, Blanche, and Arthur.

Morris was an internist practicing in Minneapolis, who tragically passed away at age 44 of a heart attack while making rounds. He was being paged and when he didn't answer, they went looking for him and found him dead. His wife was Lorraine and she later married a Minneapolis attorney. Lorraine taught chemistry at the college level at Macalester in St. Paul, and later on at Northrop Collegiate, a private school, and at a public school in Robbinsdale, MN. After Morris' death, she obtained a law degree at William Mitchell College of Law in St. Paul. As she taught during the day, she went to night school to get her degree. They have three children: Cindy, Norm, and David.

Cindy is a gastroenterologist married to Allen and they

have two children, Nathaniel and Benjamin. Nathaniel is a third-year medical student at the University of Michigan Ann Arbor, and Benjamin is in his second year of medical school at Johns Hopkins Medical School in bio-medical engineering.

Norm is married to Mitzie and they have three sons: Ben, Max, and Sam. Norm lives in Boston and is an attorney.

David is married to Carey and they have three children: Maja, Jonathon, and Hannah Rose. David has a Ph.D. from Columbia University in Pharmaceutical Chemistry and is currently on the faculty at the University of Michigan Ann Arbor.

Blanche was married to Leon Singer who had a Ph.D. in bio-chemistry from the University of Florida at Gainesville. He did research and teaching for 39 years until he retired. He passed away just three months into his retirement at age 70. Together they had five children: Eileen, Charlie, Neil, Joel, and Karen.

Eileen and Joel are both married, have children, and reside in Israel.

Charlie is a Minneapolis attorney and is married to Ann. They have three sons.

Neil is married to Jill and they have five children: Simka, a Ph.D. candidate at M.I.T. in mechanical engineering, major area being combustion; Elisha who, as I am writing this book, is finishing up his second year in medical school at the University of PA; Avinoan; Hannina; and daughter Noa. The last three are in the process of finishing their high school and middle school learning. All of their futures look extremely positive and I am happy for them.

The last of Blanche and Leon's children is Karen, who is married to Allan. They have four children.

Aunt Clara and Uncle Nathan Sherman's son Arthur is married to a woman named Patti. They have two children: Charlie and Elise. Charlie's wife Ellie recently passed away from cystic fibrosis. I believe she was in her middle 30s. What a tragedy. Ellie told Charles before they married about her condition and that she was not expected to live past 40. They met while attending Columbia University. Charlie received a $25,000 scholarship to Columbia. They adopted two children Gabe and Michael. Charlie has a nanny taking care of the kids. Charlie is currently a principal of a Jewish day school in Milwaukee.

Arthur and Patti's daughter Elise is married to Dimitri, an immigrant from Russia. They have three children and live in Chicago. They are strict Orthodox believers and follow the straight and narrow path. Patti's father was a St. Paul attorney and her mom, Bertha, was his legal secretary. Patti worked for the state and quit when she got married. Arthur had a stroke around four years ago. It's left him scared. His speech and arm and leg movements are affected. He walks a little, but mostly needs help navigating. He sometimes uses a wheelchair to move around. If it wasn't for Patti being at his side, Arthur would have to be in a nursing home.

Theirs is an interesting story of how he incurred the stroke. His cardiologist said he would have to have an angioplasty to unplug some of his arteries. Arthur is very dependent on other people. His mother-in-law Bertha, who didn't believe in surgery because of one bad outcome, demanded that he not have the procedure. After she passed, the doctor told him that if he didn't have the angioplasty he would have a massive heart attack. He was told the risks associated with that procedure and that a stroke could occur. Because he waited so long, a stroke did occur. Blanche said that had he not waited so long it might never have happened.

Arthur and Patti have always come late to events. They don't realize what an inconvenience it is for people putting on these events. I remember about two years ago they came to a Friday night supper, which I put on at Knollwood Place. It started at 6:00 p.m. Arthur and Patti arrived around one hour late. The dining room manager thought they were gate crashing and told me to pay for them. The fact was that I had paid in advance. I was embarrassed as my guests at the table I was sitting at heard the conversation between the manager and me. Last year they were on time for the Friday night supper, which shocked me.

My father's oldest uncle was Harry who was married to Rachel. They had two sons: Hymer and Morris; and a daughter Celia. All three of them were geniuses. Hymer was a radiologist and practiced in Cleveland. During the Second World War, he was the medical director of the Manhattan Project. Morris is a surgeon who started practicing at the Mayo Clinic and wound up in Chicago. He was married to the former Barbra Fishbein, whose father, Morris Fishbein, was President of the American Medical Association in the 30s and the one individual who talked President Roosevelt out of socialized medicine for America.

I met Hymer, Morris, and their wives at Uncle George's funeral. They came over to where I was sitting and introduced themselves. It proved to be the last time I would see them. Both brothers bought a building in Rochester. This occurred in the early 80s, which saw the prime interest rate jump to 21%. They tried to sell the building, but because of high interest rates, their efforts proved in vain. They then donated the building to the University of Minnesota, which then sold it the Rochester School system to house a middle school. The building is now called the Friedell Middle School and is located at 1200 South Broadway.

Celia was married to Dave, an accountant who worked for the IRS. Dave was a prince of a fellow who was easy to get along with. He was a kind of a happy-go-lucky guy. Of all my dad's cousins, I knew Celia and Dave the most because of Uncle George's efforts.

Uncle Louis lived in Lake City, MN. I believe that he was the town's refuse collector. He and his wife Yetta had two children: Morris and Clara. Morris was an accountant who at one time lived in California. Clara graduated second in her high school class and went to a business college to train as a secretary. Louis's wife committed suicide and Clara discovered her body lying in the river. Clara suffered a mental breakdown and spent 15 years at the old State Hospital in Rochester. Uncle George and Aunt Rita took her out, settled her in an apartment, and got her a job at a law firm as a legal secretary. She had several setbacks, but still managed to stay out of a state hospital. I last saw her at the nursing home where my mother was undergoing rehab for hip surgery. I met Morris for the first and only time at Uncle Louis's funeral.

My next uncle is Aaron Friedell, who was a medical doctor practicing family medicine and was married to Naomi. They had two sons: Gerry and Gilbert. Gerry is a Minneapolis attorney and lives in Minneapolis and Gilbert is a pathologist doing research at the University of Kentucky in Lexington. Gerry is married and has three children. Gilbert is married to Janet Nelson whose father, Professor

Lowry Nelson, was my major advisor at the University. It was then that I found out I was related to him.

Gilbert and Hymer were at one time listed in Who's Who in America. Uncle Aaron was many years ago named General Practitioner of the Year in Minnesota.

Next is Aunt Fanny, who was married to Ben; he passed away after being married for just a few years. She never remarried citing the reason to help Uncle George through medical school. My cousin Leon pooh-poohed that notion. She was my favorite aunt on my father's side. She spent her entire life working in garment factories in Minneapolis. Uncle George was the apple of her eye. He didn't disappoint her.

The final uncle was George Friedell, who was married to Rita, a princess of a lady who passed away from breast cancer at an early age, leaving Uncle George a widower with four children: Marion, Beverly, Cheryl, and Steve. Marion is a librarian at the master level. Beverly, who is a member of Phi Beta Kappa, is an oncologist-hematologist. Cheryl is a school teacher and Steve is an attorney. All live out east.

Of all those, Marion is the only one I never met. I met Gilbert at one of Uncle George's birthday parties. Uncle George and Aunt Rita took great pains to stay in touch with all the family, including Mom and me. I first met them in 1952 at the wedding of Blanche and Leon. They took it upon themselves to go down to Rochester to get Clara released after spending 15 years as a patient there. They rented an apartment for her at the Evangelist Building—an apartment for women that also served meals to their tenants. What a human gesture. The psychiatrist I was seeing at that time, Dr. L, was overwhelmed by Uncle

George's and Aunt Rita's caring and compassionate attitude.

In 1981, Uncle George wrote a book entitled *My Life*. In the book, he states that about six months before his father died, he said out of the clear blue sky, "George you should go to school and study medicine," citing Hymer and Morris as examples. "If these two could do it, so can you." Talk about a positive role model. The only thing Dad said to me was how he lucked out when I was born and "on your teeth" when I said something he disliked. I believe that was due to his father passing away when Dad was only three.

After Uncle George and Uncle Aaron graduated from medical school, they celebrated by going to see the Miss America Pageant in Atlantic City, New Jersey. Here you have two Russian immigrants who pursued the American dream treating themselves to a national event.

In December 1916, Uncle George was admitted to the Glen Lake Sanatorium for treatment of tuberculosis; five years later, it turned out that he was misdiagnosed. During those five years, he learned the importance of proper rest, food, and not to fear.

In the summary in *My Life*, Uncle George states:

I was ill, suffered from illness since childhood, but somehow overcame all the problems which caused my ill health in spite of the mistakes and wrong therapy used by the medical establishment. My mental state did not suffer evidently because I managed to be a good student whenever and wherever I studied. My problem was that of losing a lot of time away from the studies, but I graduated from the medical school at the age of 40 and corrected my medical condition at the age of 41 when I knew definitely what my problem was and when it was known definitely how to treat it. My philosophy eventually consisted of cause and effect; that is, everything has a cause. During my stages of growing up and getting an education, I was keen enough about the "who, what, when, where, and why." I was raised in an atmosphere where the belief was that all conditions that happened were preordained by a super natural power, but in the course of time that idea was definitely replaced by the Philosophy of Cause and Effect which is reasonable.

5.

Jobs

After my diagnosis in 1957, I was unable to return to school. Instead, I hung out in pool halls on Plymouth Avenue and in downtown Minneapolis, mainly watching the action of the players.

I would walk to the pool hall in the neighborhood and take the bus to downtown. Making time pass was my main goal.

People at the downtown pool hall who sat around were mainly retired and, like me, were trying to pass time. Some were giving me a bad time for not working. I always had the thought of going back to school to graduate with a Master's degree in social work. I had only 59 credits left to graduate at the bachelor's level before going on to grad school for a MSW. So when I felt better, I tried many times to return to school, but couldn't hold out to the finish. I cancelled many times and lost quite a bit of money in the process.

Over the years I attempted to work in order to help me support myself. The first job I had was when, after my first year in college, I went to my dad's old labor Union Local 638 Miscellaneous Drivers and Helpers to see if they knew of any job openings. My dad had passed away that February. They told me that Heinrich Envelope in Minneapolis had a temporary opening at their operation. I was hired and worked there for a couple of weeks and then was let go.

One of my duties was helping a driver named Buck. I cannot remember what my salary was back then in 1955, but it wasn't much more than a $1.50 an hour. Those were good wages in those days. That union had a $500 death benefit that members contributed to and of which my mother and I were the recipients.

One of the jobs I held was with Midwest Building Services, cleaning up an envelope company called Tension Envelope. They were owned by a Kansas City outfit with several plants around the country, including Minneapolis. The person who got me the job was Adolph Daleki, a park keeper at North Commons. I stayed there for a couple of years and then left. During that time I took a test for clerk-carrier at the Minneapolis Post Office and passed the exam with a score of 84.3. It was during the time of the Vietnam War and the Post Office was desperate for help. Carriers were delivering job notices to occupants along with their mail. I was called in for an interview and a tour. On the application form there were two questions about an applicant's health history. One was "Have you ever had a nervous breakdown or chronic condition?" As I was diagnosed with both conditions—an ulcer and mental condition—I answered yes to both questions. As I found out later from a psychiatrist, the Federal government did not hire people with a history of mental illness. Why didn't they come out and say that in their policies? Why make me go through the entire process when they have that policy? They should be open about it.

As part of the application process, I had to undergo a security investigation for a non-sensitive job. I don't know which government agency conducted the background check, either the FBI or Postal Inspectors, but I found out later what they put me through. My friend Marvin Kramer, who worked at the Minneapolis Post Office, was listed as a character reference. During my background check he was called in to tell what he knew about me. He told me that he was shown most of the material in my file. One of the things he was shown was a picture of my house that showed I did not shovel the snow. There was a lot of ice and if the snow had been shoveled off, it would have made walking on the sidewalk very treacherous. People convicted of crimes have their day in court. I never had a chance to tell my side of the story. They also checked with Minnesota Job Center to see if I was registered for work because I was unemployed at that time. I wasn't.

It has been 45 years since that incident occurred. If I was still working I could retire at a lucrative pension and not having have spent 24 years on social security disability to include 22 years on Medicare. I have often consoled myself about the embarrassment of being on disability and Medicare by saying I too have to eat.

One of the jobs I was hired at was Augsburg Publishing Company, as a packer of books and supplies to religious groups. The warehouse superintendent was a man named Grant whom I later found out in the interview was Selmer's brother. During my job hunting, I had used Selmer as a character reference, as well as the athletic director, Frank. Grant shouted out to me, "How do you know Frank?" and I told him through the American Legion Baseball program. There was always bad blood between Selmer and Frank, and evidently Grant knew about their falling out in 1953.

I was a complete flop on the job. I took only the easy books and supplies to pack, which did not suit my co-workers and that came to Grant's attention. I remember him telling me that I had 30 working days under the Union contract to improve my job performance or else I would have to leave. Shortly after that I left with no hard feelings.

I have never since that time ever used an acquaintance of mine to get a job.

In later years, after I became fully employed by the State, Mike Hatch, who had just been elected attorney general offered me a job in his agency. Remembering the past, I turned it down. I did quite a bit of volunteering for him while I was involved in politics for the DFL and he showed appreciation. He was one of the nicest people I have ever met. I remember walking by a church in St. Louis Park and they had a sign that had the name of the church, the ministers, and time of their Sunday services; and the topic of the sermon on that particular Sunday was "A Person Who Refreshes." I wish I had attended that service as a guest and listened to that sermon. I would have described Mike as a good human being—in Yiddish, a Mentsch.

Mike ran for governor several times and was defeated on all three tries. It was after that he decided to run for Attorney General, won the election, and served two terms. I remember that on election night he took us out to dinner at the Spaghetti Factory. When Mike and his family arrived, we gave them a standing ovation. I enjoyed doing volunteer work and made many friends, which I have cherished over the years.

When I was up for review on my social security I was afraid that I would be dropped because the then-President Reagan was doing a wholesale cleansing of that entitlement under the guise of saving social security. I decided to go to my congressman's office for help in obtaining a job at the Minnesota State Legislature. If I lost my entitlement, I would have lost more than a check. I would have lost Medicare too. I am alive today because of Medicare.

The person I saw that day in my congressman's office was one of his aides. She shouted out at me "We don't help anybody." For all the volunteer work I did for him, I felt I deserved a better answer as I was in dire straits.

One of jobs I held for a short period of time was at Steven Fabric Co. It was a family-owned business run by two brothers, Sol, who was called Babe, and Marvin. One of their sons also worked there. The warehouse supervisor was a fellow named Norm, a pleasant fellow. At one time, he invited two of my co-workers, Tom and Bob, up to his cabin in northern Minnesota, but not me. I felt it was bush league. I worked my tail off at that business pulling orders, doing the receiving, and occasionally sealing bags. I still remember Bob coming up to me and saying I deserved a raise and Tom felt the same way as he did. I felt this was quite a tribute to me as it never happened to me before.

Bob went on to become a member of the Fridley Police Department; law enforcement was his first love. After Tom left Steven Fabrics, he went into construction work.

The two best companies I worked for was Bachman's Floral and McGarvey Coffee. At Bachman's, my duties were to bag fertilizer and manure, and to help unload black dirt from a truck. At McGarvey, which supplied restaurants with jams and chocolate syrups, my duties included pulling orders. I also helped to put cartons on the conveyor belt for a co-worker to put cans of roasted coffee in them.

I enjoyed both jobs because of the friendliness of people around me. I felt a sense of accomplishment in a day's work. They were jobs well done. Bachman's was a temporary job, but McGarvey was a permanent position.

In March of 1971, I applied for a job at the University of Minnesota to take tickets at the Minnesota State High School Basketball tournament held at Williams Arena. I was hired and it started a 13-year career as a temporary seasonal employee; the job ended after the baseball season ended because the University hired a private security firm to do the work. I had the privilege of working all sports.

Another event was the 1974 NCAA regional baseball tournament, which was held at Siebert Field. Minnesota was in the playoffs and also hosted that event. I never saw anything like it. I don't think the stadium could seat more than 2,500 people. People just kept coming and coming. I did not go up to the stands on my break to see where they were sitting, but it must have been quite a squeeze.

My boss was named Marion and she was a princess of a lady. I got along with her on a steady basis. She was an assistant athletic ticket office manager. She treated all of us with dignity and respect. She retired some years ago and I attended her retirement party, held at the Radisson University Hotel.

Several years after I found out I was misdiagnosed, I got a letter from the Social Security regional office in Chicago asking if I was interested in obtaining help to go back to work. They were offering incentives in which I could work during a 12-month trial period without losing my benefits, including Medicare. I had already used my trial work period when I first received benefits, but collecting tickets at ball games did not constitute "substantial gainful worked activity," which they defined as working for less than a certain amount of money.

I was elated, for I was given a second chance to see if the Imipramine, which had been on the market since 1958, was going to enable me to work at a decent-paying job with excellent benefits. The program was called Project Network.

I was assigned to work with a rehabilitation company,

which had contracted to help social security disability recipients anxious to obtain employment. I was assigned to work with a caseworker who I wanted to help me. I was under the impression that it's not what you know, but who you know, if you need help—especially if you're disabled and never held a full-time job for any particular length of time. I remember reading a critique of me at the end of the program, "Mr. Friedell expects us to find a job for him." I interpreted that as being a very negative appraisal since that was their job.

The rehab company was charging the government $500 a month, but doing nothing to earn it. My counselor had a friend who worked at a local nonprofit, whom she contacted to get me a job interview. I went out to interview and never received a job offer. I felt her friend at the nonprofit just used me to keep their friendship on a solid footing. She could have gone to bat for me but chose not to do so.

After 30 months, the rehab company contract ran out and they put on a party for us. A large number of us attended. Among the speakers was the owner of the rehab firm. She told us how successful her company was in helping us out. As I looked around the room and seeing all the people still out of work, I thought to myself, "What success are you talking about?" They were screwing the government. As I was to find out in later years, Project Network was a colossal failure. The rehab company went out of business shortly after the project ended.

I had contacted the Division of Vocational Rehabilitation for the State of Minnesota and worked with a counselor named Kathy. Unlike the rehab company, she was interested in helping me obtain employment. She sent me for work evaluation at, of all places, the aforementioned nonprofit. I was evaluated and a man named Chuck, who was to be my job coach. He helped me obtain part-time employment at a collection agency.

While I was at the collection agency, I received a call from Chuck, asking me if I wanted to increase my hours, but stay at less than full-time. I told him in no uncertain terms that it was either full-time or no time. We had a heated exchange and a falling out. What he didn't understand was my burning desire to obtain full-time employment. I wanted to know if the Imipramine would allow me to work full-time and I wanted the financial security and benefits.

After that, I left the collection agency and obtained full-time employment with Target Financial as a customer service representative. During the time I worked there, I received a $5 gift certificate for outstanding customer service, which was a lot of money in those days

While at the rehab company, I took an aptitude test. It showed that I would succeed in the clerical field. Trouble with that was that times change. We are living in the age of computers. As most of my schooling was done between 1941 and 1957, I had little knowledge of computers. Still, I was determined to stay on the job, come what may. Target Financial stuck with me and I stuck with them.

My worst experience was the 4th of July weekend. As I waited for the bus to go home, I had a throbbing headache and couldn't help but think if I was able to make it through that day I could make it through any day. I felt I had the right attitude to stick on the job no matter how tough it became, and as I mentioned earlier I was recognized for outstanding customer service.

I started at an hourly salary of $6.00 per hour and later, because Target had trouble finding help, I got an increase in salary to $9.00 per hour.

* * * * * *

Since most of the people I worked with taking tickets at the University were full-time employees at the State, I always felt I, too, would like to work there. The opportunity arose. The Department of Human Services had a job opening for an enrollment rep for their Minnesota Care Division, located in St. Paul. The State had a 700-hour program for disabled people like myself. Instead of taking an exam, you get 700 hours of work experience in a particular agency of your expertise to see if you can do the work. If you are successful, you have a job, but there must be a vacancy that has to be filled.

I started in February of 1997 as an enrollment rep. It was difficult for me to learn the Minnesota Care Program. It is a medical insurance program beset with many difficult tasks. I had difficulty learning the mechanics of the program and my 700 hours were almost up. Linda, my supervisor at that time, asked me if I was interested in demoting to being a clerical. I jumped at the opportunity and transferred over to that side. If it wasn't for Linda, I would have been out of a job and back on the street. The memory of what she did for me will last me a lifetime and means a great deal to me. She is a kind and considerate person and I will always be grateful to her.

My duties as a clerical included opening mail and date stamping applications and proofs of income, such as W2's and federal income tax forms, picking up mail from the reps, filing client folders in the retriever, and serving as a backup receptionist in the early morning hours. My supervisor was a lady named Peg. She could rely on me to always be on time as punctuality and patience are some of my virtues. I always felt comfortable in handling phones. I got my start on phones as a volunteer in the Don Fraser mayoral campaign in 1979.

The mail we received would go from the St. Paul Post

Office to our main facility on Lafayette Road and come to us at 8 E. 4th Street in downtown St. Paul. We opened at 7:00 a.m. and we didn't get the mail from our main facility until 10:00 a.m., a three-hour delay. I pleaded with Peg to have the mail come directly to our building, as it was not our job to deliver the mail, it is the Post Office's job. This was, in my opinion, a miscue, especially at the last day of the month, which we called cut-off day. If we didn't get people's renewal application in by that day they were out of the program. This was a serious matter as they would lose their coverage for two months. I pleaded with Peg to get the mail 7:00 a.m., but to no avail.

During my eight years, I had the good fortune of meeting many interesting people, as we employed 150 people. There was Georgia, who had a heart of gold, but made sure you did the work her way or else. I remember her telling another co-worker that she wanted to lend her money because of the difficulty my co-worker was having in fulfilling her financial obligations. How many people would do that? Only Georgia could do that.

Besides Georgia, I worked with Tam, who came to America in 1975 from Vietnam. I remember when expressing an opinion I'd turn to Tam and would say to her "right, Tam," and she would say "right on, right on" in her foreign accent. I enjoyed their company.

Then there was Kerry, who would sell her own mother out if the opportunity arose. She was a higher-level clerical whom management would listen to. In one instance, she told an assistant manager that I was reading applications. This was against Data Privacy laws. The information I read never got out of our secured area. I remember receiving an application from a person who was diagnosed with tuberculosis as stated on the application. Tuberculosis is a contagious disease. What if I didn't read the application and contracted T.B. as it was called? I reported it to management so that precautionary measures could be taken. Happily everything turned out positively. The assistant manager told me if I got caught reading applications again I would be disciplined. I wish Kerry could have kept quiet but she was that kind of person.

Mike, our security man, told me when people would come in to fill out applications and they needed help, a rep would come down to help them. This was done behind closed doors to maintain privacy. The problem came when reps would leave the room with the clients, they unwittingly discussed the case in an unsecured area on the 7th floor. People that are waiting to get help heard their conversations. As Kerry did not witness what was going on, those reps were never called on the carpet like I was.

During one year, I asked Peg to approve vacation leave for me for Rash Hashanah and Yom Kipper. She refused my request. So I emailed the lady who was the director of the office of diversity and equal opportunity to ask for help in obtaining a leave so I could attend services. I told her we are forced to attend workshops in diversity. She told me their lectures fall on deaf ears no matter how hard they try. She told me that she would go to our manager, Mary Jo, to tell her my dilemma, but needed my permission to do so. I refused to give her permission to do so as I believed she would grant my request, which she eventually did. There was no rhyme or reason why my request for leave could not have been immediately approved. That's what decent people do, but in Peg's case, it was asking too much.

Several years ago, at the request of a state legislator, the Minnesota Legislative Auditor investigated the Minnesota Care Program. In 2005, four of us were terminated from our jobs as office specialists for no apparent reason. This was in spite of hiring at the next level—Clerk 2. Why not train us to that work so we would not lose our jobs? That was asking too much of management.

I retired at that time and, largely thanks to Linda, I am receiving a state pension, social security, old age deferred comp (401K), and a couple of IRAs, so I have some financial security.

Conclusion

This is my story. I have attempted to put bits and pieces together to form a whole. Dr. Heefner, during one of my visits, asked me what I would do differently had I not been misdiagnosed. I told him that I would have finished my schooling. After obtaining a Master's degree in social work, I would have worked as a probation officer or parole agent in the public sector. If that was not possible, I wanted to work in the private sector, such as the United Way, in the area of social gerontology.

Number 2, I would have served in the military. The draft was going on and I'm not a draft dodger.

Number 3, I would have established a career.

And number 4, I would have married and raised a family.

All this passed me by because of betrayal by my parents and the mental health system. It resulted in shattered hopes, shattered dreams. Since the start of the abuse, beating with the belt by my father, I believed I had it coming. The episode that awoke me and made me question the propriety of the beatings were the headlines in the *Minneapolis Star Tribune*, two of which read on Tuesday, May 26, 1987: "Abuse was Part of Daily Life in Jurgens' Household," and an article which appeared on Wednesday, May 13, 1987 entitled, "Prosecutor says Jurgens Beat Child from Outset. Defense Admits Pattern of Abuse." In reading over all the articles, I found out that the remaining of her adopted children required the services of mental health professionals the same as me. What an awakening.

When I showed the articles to Mom, she showed some emotion, but she became hardened in the fact that I had it coming because I irritated Dad.

Lois Jurgens was found guilty of murder and served eight years at the Minnesota Woman's Reformatory in Shakopee.

The abuse I suffered resulted in me spending 33 years on the street living with fear of swallowing and the fear of being in large crowds, such as in an auditorium, where I was seated far from a door.

This all ended on April 16, 1991, when I sought the services of Dr. Heefner who told me I was not schizophrenic. An article appeared on the front page of the *Minneapolis Star Tribune* that a new drug had been found for treating schizophrenia. This article turned my life around.

The question arises of what kept me going those 33 years on the street: (1) patience; (2) tomorrow would be better; (3) a sense of humor; and (4) the ability to laugh at myself.

One important point I want to make is that anyone who is abused should tell a person who can be trusted—such as a teacher, a social worker, doctor, clergy, or a nurse—about the abuse so they can help. Everyone deserves to fulfill a promising future and not wind up like I did. Never tell a classmate as all this information should be confidential.

Never assume, as I did, that you have it coming.

About the Author

Marshall Friedell is a retired public clerk. He lives in
Hopkins, Minnesota and is happily enjoying his
good health, both mental and physical.

Made in the USA
Monee, IL
28 November 2020

49905877R00056